Math Contests
Grades 7 and 8
Volume 1

School Years
1977-78 through 1981-82

Written by

Steven R. Conrad • Daniel Flegler

Published by MATH LEAGUE PRESS
Printed in the United States of America

Cover art by Bob DeRosa

Second Printing, 1997

Copyright © 1992, 1997
by Mathematics Leagues Inc.
All Rights Reserved

Math League Press
P.O. Box 720
Tenafly, NJ 07670-0720

ISBN 0-940805-07-3

Preface

Math Contests—Grades 7 and 8, Volume 1 is the first volume in our series of problem books for grades 7 and 8. This volume contain the contests given in the school years 1977-78 through 1981-82 The second and third volumes contain the contests given from 1982-83 through 1995-96, as well as the Algebra Course 1 Contests given from 1993-94 through 1995-96. (You can use the order form on page 94 to order any of our 9 books.)

This book is divided into three sections for ease of use by students and teachers. You'll find the contests in the first section. Each contest consists of 40 multiple-choice questions that you can do in 30 minutes. On each 3-page contest, the questions on the 1st page are generally straightforward, those on the 2nd page are moderate in difficulty, and those on the 3rd page are more difficult. In the second section of the book, you'll find detailed solutions to all the contest questions. In the third and final section of the book are the letter answers to each contest. In this section, you'll also find rating scales you can use to rate your performance.

Many people prefer to consult the answer section rather than the solution section when first reviewing a contest. We believe that reworking a problem when you know the answer (but *not* the solution) often leads to increased understanding of problem-solving techniques.

Each school year, we sponsor an Annual 7th Grade Mathematics Contest, an Annual 8th Grade Mathematics Contest, and an Annual Algebra Course 1 Mathematics Contest. A student may participate in the contest on grade level or for any higher grade level. For example, students in grade 7 (or below) may participate in the 8th Grade Contest. *Any* student may participate in the Algebra Course 1 Contest. Starting with the 1991-92 school year, students have been permitted to use calculators on any of our contests.

Steven R. Conrad & Daniel Flegler, contest authors

Acknowledgments

For her continued patience and understanding, special thanks to Marina Conrad, whose only mathematical skill, an important one, is the ability to count the ways.

For her lifetime support and encouragement, special thanks to Mildred Flegler.

To Alan Feldman, who proofread this book, thanks!

Table Of Contents

The Contests

• •

1977-78 through 1981-82

1977-78 Annual 7th Grade Contest

Tuesday, February 14, 1978

7

Instructions

- **Time** You will have only *30 minutes* working time for this contest. You might be *unable* to finish all 40 questions in the time allowed.

- **Scores** Please remember that *this is a contest, not a test*—and there is no "passing" or "failing" score. Few students score as high as 30 points (75% correct). Students with half that, 15 points, *should be commended!*

- **Format and Point Value** This is a multiple-choice contest. Every answer is an A, B, C, or D. For each question, write your answer in the *Answers* column to the right of the question. A correct answer is worth 1 point. Unanswered questions get no credit.

1. The product of the digits 1, 2, 3, 4, 5, 6, 7, 8, 9, and 0 is | 1.
   A) 5040   B) 40320   C) 362880   D) none of these

2. To the nearest tenth, 8.849 = | 2.
   A) 8.85   B) 8.8   C) 8.9   D) none of these

3. The intersection of the sets {1, 3, 5, 7} and {1, 2, 3} is | 3.
   A) {1,2,3,5,7}   B) {1}   C) $\varnothing$ D) none of these

4. $\dfrac{0.42}{0.014} =$ | 4.

   A) 0.03   B) 0.3   C) 3   D) 30

5. The product $3141 \times 243 = 7?3263$ will be correct when ? is replaced by | 5.
   A) 6   B) 8   C) 9   D) none of these

6. What percent of 44 is 55? | 6.
   A) 125%   B) 120%   C) 80%   D) 75%

7. If the sum of two numbers is 10, their product is at most | 7.
   A) 9   B) 10   C) 25   D) none of these

8. The perimeter of a square is 32. The area of this square is | 8.
   A) 16   B) 32   C) 64   D) none of these

9. The whole numbers have the commutative property under | 9.
   I. Addition   II. Multiplication
   A) only I   B) only II   C) I and II   D) none of these

10. Of 1, 11, 21, 31, 41, and 51, how many are prime numbers? | 10.
    A) 3   B) 4   C) 5   D) none of these

11. If d is the length of a circle's diameter, the circle's area is | 11.
    A) $\dfrac{\pi d^2}{4}$ B) $\dfrac{\pi d^2}{2}$ C) πd^2 D) $2\pi d$

12. The smallest prime number greater than 90 is | 12.
    A) 91   B) 93   C) 97   D) none of these

13. 12 is what percent of 80? | 13.
    A) 30%   B) 20%   C) 15%   D) none of these

14. $(6 \times 10^4) + (5 \times 10^2) + (3 \times 10^1) =$ | 14.
    A) 653   B) 6053   C) 356   D) none of these

15. Set S has exactly one subset. How many elements are in set S? | 15.
    A) 0   B) 1   C) 2   D) none of these

Go on to the next page IIII➡ **7**

2

16. When $4\frac{1}{6}$ is divided by $1\frac{2}{3}$, the quotient is

 A) $2\frac{1}{2}$ B) $\frac{2}{5}$ C) $2\frac{1}{5}$ D) none of these

16.

17. Which shows that multiplication is distributive over addition?
 A) $3(4 \times 5) = (3 \times 4)(3 \times 5)$ B) $3(4 + 5) = 3(5 + 4)$
 C) $3(4 \times 5) = 3 \times 4 \times 5$ D) none of these

17.

18. $8 \div 2 \times 4 =$

 A) 64   B) 16   C) 4   D) 1

18.

19. In a class of 30, 12 are boys. If 6 more boys are admitted, what part of the class is then boys?

 A) $\frac{1}{3}$ B) $\frac{1}{2}$ C) $\frac{2}{5}$ D) none of these

19.

20. In the base six numeral 3254, the digit 2 represents the number
 A) 36   B) 72   C) 200   D) 216

20.

21. $4 + 3 \times 5 - 2 =$

 A) 13   B) 21   C) 33   D) none of these

21.

22. A tennis player won 6 out of 12 matches and then won the next 6 matches. What percent of the matches did she win?

 A) $\frac{2}{3}\%$ B) 50%   C) $66\frac{2}{3}\%$ D) none of these

22.

23. Find the ratio of 9.6 to 8.
 A) 6:5   B) 12:1   C) 1:12   D) none of these

23.

24. Find the least common multiple of 14, 21, and 42.
 A) 7   B) $14 \times 21 \times 42$ C) 42   D) none of these

24.

25. If a number is tripled and then divided by $\frac{1}{2}$, the result is the same as multiplying the original number by

 A) $\frac{3}{2}$ B) $\frac{2}{3}$ C) 6   D) none of these

25.

26. The number 56 is $87\frac{1}{2}\%$ of

 A) 35   B) 49   C) 64   D) none of these

26.

27. In a right triangle, if the lengths of the legs are 10 and 24, the length of the hypotenuse is
 A) 17   B) 26   C) 34   D) 38

27.

28. How many of the numbers 0, 4, 6 are even numbers?
 A) 0   B) 1   C) 2   D) 3

28.

29. If A and B are sets whose union is B, then it *must* be true that
 A) A is a subset of B B) $A = \varnothing$
 C) $A = B$ D) none of these

29.

Go on to the next page ▐▌▌⮕ **7**

3

30. The difference between a 2-digit number and the number with its digits reversed is *always* divisible by A) 2 B) 4 C) 6 D) none of these	30.
31. At the rate of 3 grams for 65¢, for $11.70 I can buy A) 18 grams B) 54 grams C) 62 grams D) none of these	31.
32. When expressed as a percent, $0.03\frac{1}{3}$ becomes A) $33\frac{1}{3}\%$ B) $3\frac{1}{3}\%$ C) $0.03\frac{1}{3}\%$ D) none of these	32.
33. The number 124150.5225 is the square of a number which has ? non-zero digits to the right of its decimal point. A) 2 B) 3 C) 4 D) 5	33.
34. A shopper can choose to have a discount of 18%, followed by a discount of 23%; or the shopper can choose to have the order of the discounts reversed. The first method gives a final price which is ? when compared to the final price obtained by reversing the order of the discounts. A) cheaper B) more expensive C) the same D) none of these	34.
35. A man spent two-thirds of his money and misplaced two-thirds of the remainder, leaving him with $18. With how much money did he start? A) $42 B) $50 C) $81 D) none of these	35.
36. At the rate of $450 for 38 suitcases, 57 suitcases will cost A) $674.88 B) $675.45 C) $684.00 D) none of these	36.
37. An example of numbers written in *increasing* order is A) $\frac{11}{15}, \frac{13}{19}, \frac{13}{23}$ B) $\frac{13}{23}, \frac{13}{19}, \frac{11}{15}$ C) $\frac{13}{23}, \frac{11}{15}, \frac{13}{19}$ D) none of these	37.
38. Of the following, the one with the cheapest price per gram is A) $1\frac{3}{4}$ grams for 19¢ B) $2\frac{5}{6}$ grams for 39¢ C) $5\frac{3}{7}$ grams for 79¢ D) 1 gram for 12¢	38.
39. $2 + \dfrac{1}{3+\frac{1}{4}}$ is equivalent to A) $3\frac{1}{4}$ B) $2\frac{4}{13}$ C) $2\frac{1}{13}$ D) none of these	39.
40. Engraving costs 62¢ for the first 5 letters and 8¢ for each additional letter. How many letters are there in a name which costs $1.66 to engrave? A) 13 B) 18 C) 20 D) none of these	40.

The end of the contest **7**

Solutions on Page 41 · Answers on Page 82

1978-79 Annual 7th Grade Contest

Tuesday, February 13, 1979

7

Instructions

- **Time** You will have only *30 minutes* working time for this contest. You might be *unable* to finish all 40 questions in the time allowed.

- **Scores** Please remember that *this is a contest, not a test*—and there is no "passing" or "failing" score. Few students score as high as 30 points (75% correct). Students with half that, 15 points, *should be commended!*

- **Format and Point Value** This is a multiple-choice contest. Every answer is an A, B, C, or D. For each question, write your answer in the *Answers* column to the right of the question. A correct answer is worth 1 point. Unanswered questions get no credit.

1.	41.7 − 32.8 =		1.
	A) 74.5 B) 9.1 C) 11.1 D) 8.9		

2. What percent of the diagram at the right is shaded?   2.

    A) 18%   B) $\frac{3}{16}$%   C) $18\frac{3}{4}$%   D) 3%

3. When _?_ is divided by 3, the quotient is 6 and the remainder is 0.   3.

    A) 18   B) 9   C) 3   D) 2

4. Find 5% of 2400.   4.

    A) 1200   B) 120   C) 24   D) 12

5. When $\frac{8}{9}$ is divided by $\frac{4}{3}$, the result is   5.

    A) $\frac{32}{27}$ B) $\frac{2}{3}$ C) $\frac{2}{27}$ D) 6

6. In a right triangle, if one acute angle has a measure of 48°, the other acute angle has a measure of   6.

    A) 42°   B) 52°   C) 90°   D) 132°

7. 0.2×0.3 =   7.

    A) 0.006   B) 0.06   C) 0.6   D) 6

8. Find the remainder when 2 000 000 000 001 is divided by 3.   8.

    A) 0   B) 1   C) 2   D) 4

9. $\frac{0.015}{0.03} =$ 9.

    A) 0.005   B) 0.05   C) 0.5   D) 5

10. Find the average of the 1000 whole numbers from 1 to 1000 inclusive.   10.

    A) 499.5   B) 500.0   C) 500.5   D) 501.0

11. Find the ratio of 15 centimeters to 3 meters.   11.

    A) 1:20   B) 1:5   C) 5:1   D) 20:1

12. How many whole numbers are divisors of 12?   12.

    A) two   B) three   C) four   D) six

13. 10 + 20 ÷ 2 + 3 =   13.

    A) 6   B) 14   C) 18   D) 23

14. 2.97×4.13 is most nearly equal to   14.

    A) 120   B) 12   C) 1.2   D) 0.12

15. If the area of a square is 64, its perimeter is   15.

    A) 256   B) 128   C) 64   D) 32

16. $\frac{1}{2} + \frac{1}{25} =$ 16.

    A) 0.50   B) 0.52   C) 0.54   D) 0.56

Go on to the next page ⮞ **7**

17. The least common multiple of 6, 8, 10, and 12 is

    A) 360   B) 240   C) 60   D) 120

    17.

18. A tennis player uses up 800 calories every hour. In 1 hour and 15 minutes, how many calories does this player use?

    A) 900   B) 1000   C) 1100   D) 1200

    18.

19. How many positive prime numbers are divisible by 17?

    A) 0   B) 1   C) 2   D) 3

    19.

20. The number 6 is what percent of 15?

    A) 25%   B) 30%   C) 40%   D) 60%

    20.

21. Of the following, which has the largest value?

    A) 2^{10} B) 3^4 C) 4^3 D) 10^2

    21.

22. Of the 90% of students in a math class who got a passing grade, 10% got $B+$ or better. What percent of the entire math class received $B+$ or better?

    A) 7%   B) 8%   C) 9%   D) 10%

    22.

23. If today is Tuesday, what day of the week will it be 365 days from today?

    A) Monday   B) Tuesday   C) Wednesday D) Thursday

    23.

24. If two straight lines intersect as shown, then $x° + y° =$

    A) 20°   B) 40°   C) 80°   D) 180°

    24.

25. The expression $\dfrac{\frac{1}{2} + \frac{1}{3}}{\frac{1}{2} - \frac{1}{3}}$ is equivalent to

    A) $\frac{1}{6}$ B) 1   C) $\frac{5}{6}$ D) 5

    25.

26. When a 3-digit integer is multiplied by a 3-digit integer, the product *may* have

    A) 3 digits   B) 4 digits   C) 6 digits   D) 9 digits

    26.

27. $2\frac{1}{2} \times 3\frac{3}{4} \times 5\frac{1}{3} =$

    A) 50   B) $31\frac{7}{12}$ C) $30\frac{1}{8}$ D) $11\frac{7}{12}$

    27.

28. $\frac{1}{4}$ is the square root of

    A) $\frac{1}{2}$ B) $\frac{1}{4}$ C) $\frac{1}{8}$ D) $\frac{1}{16}$

    28.

29. A girl walks $\frac{3}{4}$ of the way home in 18 minutes. At the same rate, she can walk the rest of the way home in

    A) $4\frac{1}{2}$ minutes B) 6 minutes   C) 9 minutes   D) 24 minutes

    29.

Go on to the next page ⫸ **7**

30. If the circumferences of two circles are in the ratio 2:3, then their areas are in the ratio

    A) 2:3   B) 2:5   C) 3:5   D) 4:9

    30.

31. How much larger than $\frac{1}{9}$ of 3 is $\frac{2}{5}$ of $1\frac{2}{3}$?

    A) $\frac{2}{25}$ B) $\frac{1}{6}$ C) $\frac{1}{3}$ D) $\frac{18}{25}$

    31.

32. A girl had 20 coins in nickels and dimes whose sum was $1.40. She spent 65¢, using 8 coins. She now has ? nickels.

    A) 7   B) 9   C) 11   D) 12

    32.

33. A recipe calls for 1 cup of flour for every $\frac{2}{3}$ cup of sugar. If 1 cup of sugar is used, then how much flour should be used?

    A) 1 cup   B) $1\frac{1}{8}$ cups   C) $1\frac{1}{4}$ cups   D) $1\frac{1}{2}$ cups

    33.

34. A boy's test grades are 68, 72, 78, 80, and 86. What grade must he get on his next test to make his test average exactly 75?

    A) 66   B) 68   C) 71   D) 75

    34.

35. In which of the following arrangements are the numbers placed in increasing size order?

    A) $\frac{7}{11}, \frac{5}{8}, \frac{3}{5}, \frac{2}{3}$ B) $\frac{3}{5}, \frac{5}{8}, \frac{2}{3}, \frac{7}{11}$ C) $\frac{3}{5}, \frac{5}{8}, \frac{7}{11}, \frac{2}{3}$ D) $\frac{2}{3}, \frac{3}{5}, \frac{5}{8}, \frac{7}{11}$

    35.

36. Jack picks 3 liters of berries in 8 minutes. Jill picks 4 liters of berries in 10 minutes. Working together, how many berries can they pick in 1 minute?

    A) $\frac{7}{9}$ B) $\frac{7}{18}$ C) $\frac{8}{19}$ D) $\frac{31}{40}$

    36.

37. In a 36-minute gym period, 24 boys want to play basketball. If only 10 can play at the same time, and each boy plays the same amount of time, how many minutes does each boy play?

    A) 12   B) 15   C) 18   D) 20

    37.

38. The lengths of the sides of a triangle are 6, 8, and 10. The area of this triangle is

    A) 24   B) 30   C) 40   D) 48

    38.

39. Of 50 people, 38 have brown hair, 29 have brown eyes, and 23 have both brown hair and brown eyes. How many have neither brown hair nor brown eyes?

    A) 6   B) 8   C) 10   D) 12

    39.

40. In a 10-team league, each team plays every other team exactly twice. Find the total number of games played in the league.

    A) 20   B) 45   C) 90   D) 180

    40.

The end of the contest ✍ **7**

Solutions on Page 45 · Answers on Page 83

1979-80 Annual 7th Grade Contest

Tuesday, February 12, 1980

7

Instructions

- **Time** You will have only *30 minutes* working time for this contest. You might be *unable* to finish all 40 questions in the time allowed.

- **Scores** Please remember that *this is a contest, not a test*—and there is no "passing" or "failing" score. Few students score as high as 30 points (75% correct). Students with half that, 15 points, *should be commended!*

- **Format and Point Value** This is a multiple-choice contest. Every anThis is a multiple-choice contest. Every answer is an A, B, C, or D. For each question, write your answer in the *Answers* column to the right of the question. A correct answer is worth 1 point. Unanswered questions get no credit.

Copyright © 1980 by Mathematics Leagues Inc.

9

		Answers
1. $4444 - 444 + 44 - 4 =$ A) 4936 B) 4040 C) 3960 D) 3952		1.
2. Which is nearest in value to 8? A) 8.1 B) 8.01 C) 8.005 D) 7.985		2.
3. $6\frac{3}{4} + 2\frac{1}{2} =$ A) $9\frac{1}{4}$ B) 9 C) $8\frac{3}{4}$ D) $8\frac{1}{4}$		3.
4. If the measure of one angle of a right triangle is 70°, the smallest angle of the triangle has a measure of A) 1° B) 10° C) 15° D) 20°		4.
5. $\frac{7}{9} =$ A) $\frac{7-2}{9-2}$ B) $\frac{7 \times 7}{9 \times 9}$ C) $\frac{7+2}{9+2}$ D) $\frac{7 \times 2}{9 \times 2}$		5.
6. Last June, it rained 10% of the days. Last June it rained on A) 10 days B) 6 days C) 3 days D) no days		6.
7. $\frac{-3}{10} \times \frac{-5}{6} =$ A) $\frac{1}{4}$ B) $\frac{1}{2}$ C) 2 D) 4		7.
8. The number of different positive two-digit whole numbers is A) 90 B) 91 C) 99 D) 89		8.
9. Find the missing number: $25 + 250 = 25 \times \underline{\ ?\ }$ A) 10 B) 11 C) 25 D) 250		9.
10. $\frac{1 + 2 + 3 + 4 + 5}{2 + 4 + 6 + 8 + 10} =$ A) $\frac{1}{32}$ B) $\frac{1}{15}$ C) $\frac{1}{2}$ D) 1		10.
11. In the *subtraction* problem shown at the right, the two ?'s represent missing digits. The *sum* of these two missing digits is A) 10 B) 9 C) 8 D) 7	?1? − 347	11. 563
12. $0.1 \times 0.2 \times 0.3 =$ A) 0.0006 B) 0.006 C) 0.06 D) 0.6		12.
13. A diagonal divides a square into two triangles, each of which has an area of 18 cm². The perimeter of the square is A) 18 cm B) 20 cm C) 24 cm D) 36 cm		13.
14. 20% of 60 = 30% of A) 40 B) 50 C) 90 D) 100		14.
15. $2 + 6 \times 6 - 3 \times 2 + 1 =$ A) 29 B) 33 C) 39 D) 91		15.

Go on to the next page ⮕ **7**

16. How many whole numbers are divisors of 36?   16.
   A) 6   B) 7   C) 8   D) 9

17. Which fraction has the smallest value?   17.
   A) $\frac{0.2}{5}$ B) $\frac{2}{0.5}$ C) $\frac{0.2}{0.5}$ D) $\frac{0.5}{2}$

18. A triangle can have sides whose lengths are 9 cm, 16 cm, and   18.
   A) 7 cm   B) 8 cm   C) 25 cm   D) 26 cm

19. The units' digit of the sum $1980^2 + 1981^2 + 1982^2$ is   19.
   A) 3   B) 4   C) 5   D) 6

20. The average of four numbers is 20. The average of these same four numbers and 15 is   20.
   A) 17   B) 19   C) 21   D) 23

21. Find the quotient: $567\overline{)567\,567\,567\,567}$.   21.
   A) 4   B) 1 111   C) 1 010 101   D) 1 001 001 001

22. Carole now has 4 times as many tapes as she had last year. She has 64 tapes now. Last year, the number of tapes she had was   22.
   A) 16   B) 32   C) 48   D) 256

23. The square root of 0.0009 is   23.
   A) 0.0003   B) 0.003   C) 0.03   D) 0.3

24. The figure at the right consists of five squares of the same size. The area of the figure is 180. The perimeter of the figure is   24.
   A) 36   B) 45   C) 72   D) 120

25. $3^3 + 3^3 + 3^3$ 25.
   A) 9^9 B) 9^3 C) 3^9 D) 3^4

26. If two consecutive odd numbers are both primes, they are called *twin primes*. One example of a pair of *twin primes* is   26.
   A) 19 and 21   B) 39 and 41   C) 49 and 51   D) 59 and 61

27. Of the following, the one with the largest value is   27.
   A) $\frac{7}{9}$ B) $\frac{5}{9}$ C) $\frac{8}{11}$ D) $\frac{9}{12}$

28. A 34 m ladder is leaning against a wall. Its base is 16 m from the wall. How many meters up the wall does the ladder reach?   28.
   A) 24   B) 26   C) 28   D) 30

29. $\frac{1}{9}$ is closest in value to   29.
   A) $\frac{4}{40}$ B) $\frac{5}{40}$ C) $\frac{6}{40}$ D) $\frac{7}{40}$

Go on to the next page ⫸ **7**

30. Al calls every 3 days, Lee every 4 days, and Pat every 6 days. Once in every _?_ days, all three will call on the same day. A) 9 B) 12 C) 13 D) 15	30.
31. Find the missing number: $33.4 : 334 = \underline{\ ?\ } : 33.4$ A) 0.0334 B) 0.334 C) 3.34 D) 334	31.
32. A shopkeeper makes a profit of 20% of the selling price of an article. The percent profit the shopkeeper makes on the cost is A) 20% B) 25% C) 40% D) 80%	32.
33. The symbol 5! represents the product of the first 5 positive whole numbers. The value of 5! + 5 is A) 10 B) 25 C) 29 D) 125	33.
34. Find the units' digit of 27^{27}. A) 1 B) 3 C) 7 D) 9	34.
35. A *Norman Window* is in the shape of a rectangle topped by a semicircle. If the shorter side of the rectangle is 6 and its longer side is 8, the perimeter of the window is A) $22 + 18\pi$ B) $22 + 9\pi$ C) $22 + 6\pi$ D) $22 + 3\pi$	35.
36. $\cfrac{1}{2 + \cfrac{3}{4 + \frac{5}{6}}}$ is equivalent to A) $\frac{29}{20}$ B) $\frac{20}{29}$ C) $\frac{29}{76}$ D) $\frac{76}{29}$	36.
37. Twelve 5-liter cans, filled with syrup, weigh a total of 492 units. Each can, when empty, weighs 3 units. The weight of 1 liter of syrup alone (*without* a can) is most nearly A) 5 units B) 6.5 units C) 7.5 units D) 8 units	37.
38. If $a * b$ means $\frac{a+b}{2}$, find the value of $(9 * 15) * 24$. A) 24 B) 18 C) 16 D) 12	38.
39. The length of a radius of a circle is decreased by 10%. This causes the area to be decreased by A) 19% B) 20% C) 21% D) 25%	39.
40. A man has 2 pennies, 3 nickels, 1 dime, and 2 quarters. How many different *sums* of money can he make using one or more of these 8 coins? A) 8 B) 12 C) 47 D) 77	40.

The end of the contest 🖎 **7**

Solutions on Page 49 · Answers on Page 84

12

1980-81 Annual 7th Grade Contest

Tuesday, February 10, 1981

7

Instructions

■ **Time** You will have only *30 minutes* working time for this contest. You might be *unable* to finish all 40 questions in the time allowed.

■ **Scores** Please remember that *this is a contest, not a test*—and there is no "passing" or "failing" score. Few students score as high as 30 points (75% correct). Students with half that, 15 points, *should be commended!*

■ **Format and Point Value** This is a multiple-choice contest. Every answer is an A, B, C, or D. For each question, write your answer in the *Answers* column to the right of the question. A correct answer is worth 1 point. Unanswered questions get no credit.

Answers

1. 8642 + 2468 A) 10000 B) 10010 C) 10110 D) 11110	1.
2. $3\frac{3}{5}$ = A) $\frac{36}{10}$ B) $\frac{18}{10}$ C) $\frac{4}{5}$ D) 3.3	2.
3. Find the units' digit in the product: 3759×9573 A) 9 B) 7 C) 5 D) 3	3.
4. 0.66 − 0.6 = A) 6.0 B) 0.6 C) 0.06 D) 0.006	4.
5. (1 + 2 + 3 + 4 + 5) + (95 + 96 + 97 + 98 + 99) = A) 100 B) 498 C) 499 D) 500	5.
6. Write as a decimal: ninety and seven hundredths A) 790.0 B) 90.7 C) 90.07 D) 0.97	6.
7. Which is *not* a prime number? A) 107 B) 87 C) 67 D) 47	7.
8. 1% of $23000 = A) $0.023 B) $23 C) $230 D) $2300	8.
9. The measure of the complement of $\angle A$ is 25°. The measure of $\angle A$ is A) 25° B) 65° C) 75° D) 155°	9.
10. 0.03×0.02 = A) 0.6 B) 0.06 C) 0.006 D) 0.0006	10.
11. The greatest common factor of 16 and 24 is A) 4 B) 8 C) 48 D) 384	11.
12. $\frac{20 \times 30 \times 40}{2 \times 3 \times 4}$ = A) 1000 B) 300 C) 30 D) 10	12.
13. Steve reads 20 pages in 50 minutes. At that rate, how long will it take him to read 50 pages? A) 20 min B) 1 hr 20 min C) 1 hr 45 min D) 2 hr 5 min	13.
14. Which of the following numbers is *not* a factor of 6420? A) 7 B) 5 C) 3 D) 2	14.
15. 60 meters of fencing are needed to fence in a square lot. What is the area of the lot? A) 3600 m^2 B) 900 m^2 C) 225 m^2 D) 15 m^2	15.
16. Divide 43.416 by 0.06. A) 7.236 B) 72.36 C) 723.6 D) 7236.0	16.

Go on to the next page ▭▶ **7**

Answers

---

17. In a school of 300 students, 27 were absent. What percent of the students were absent?

A) 9% B) 27% C) 81% D) 91%

17.

---

18. $\frac{1}{4}$ of 5 hours 20 minutes is

A) 1 hr 15 min B) 1 hr 20 min C) 1 hr 35 min D) 1 hr 40 min

18.

---

19. $1^9 + 1^{10} + 1^{11} =$

A) 1^{30} B) 3^1 C) 3^{10} D) 3^{30}

19.

---

20. The ratio of the diameters of two circles is 1:4. The ratio of their radii is

A) 1:2 B) 1:4 C) 1:8 D) 1:16

20.

---

21. $0.87\frac{1}{2} + \frac{1}{8} =$

A) 1 B) $0.99\frac{1}{2}$ C) $0.95\frac{1}{2}$ D) $0.87\frac{5}{8}$

21.

---

22. Two dozen eggs at 89¢ per dozen are paid for with a $10 bill. The proper change is

A) $1.78 B) $7.22 C) $8.22 D) $9.11

22.

---

23. $\frac{1}{7} + \frac{1}{70} + \frac{1}{700} =$

A) $\frac{1}{777}$ B) $\frac{3}{777}$ C) $\frac{100}{777}$ D) $\frac{111}{700}$

23.

---

24. The angles of a triangle are in the ratio 1:2:3. The measure of the largest angle of this triangle is

A) 30° B) 60° C) 90° D) 120°

24.

---

25. 25% of 50% of 100 is

A) 12½ B) 25 C) 50 D) 75

25.

---

26. A car left from Uphere at 9:00 A.M. and arrived at Downthere, 340 km away, at 1:15 P.M. the same day. Find the average speed of the car in kilometers per hour.

A) $\frac{340}{7.75}$ B) $\frac{340}{255}$ C) $\frac{340}{415}$ D) $\frac{340}{4.25}$

26.

---

27. The reciprocal of $\left(\frac{1}{3} + \frac{1}{4}\right)$ is

A) 7 B) $\frac{7}{3}$ C) $\frac{4}{3}$ D) $\frac{12}{7}$

27.

---

28. On a certain test, six students scored 75, seven scored 80, eight scored 85, and nine scored 90. What is the overall average of all these students?

A) 80 B) 82½ C) 83⅓ D) 84

28.

---

29. If $\frac{2}{3} \blacksquare \frac{3}{2} = 1$, then $\blacksquare$ really represents the operation

A) × B) ÷ C) + D) −

29.

Go on to the next page ⫸ 7

15

30. Which of the following does *not* represent the lengths of the sides of a right triangle? A) 3, 4, 5 B) 4, 5, 6 C) 6, 8, 10 D) 5, 12, 13	30.
31. $\sqrt{1^3 + 2^3 + 3^3 + 4^3} =$ A) 5 B) 10 C) 100 D) $\sqrt{1000}$	31.
32. Find the missing number: $\frac{6}{5} \times 70 = 1\frac{1}{3} \times$ <u>?</u> A) 60 B) 63 C) 84 D) 112	32.
33. In the figure, PSQ is a straight line, and $\overline{RS} \perp \overline{ST}$. If the measure of $\angle RSQ$ is 48°, find the measure of $\angle PST$? A) 132° B) 134° C) 136° D) 138°	33.
34. The scale of a certain map is ¾ inch = 12 miles. A park is represented on this map by a square whose side is ⅝ inch. Find the actual area of this park in square miles. A) 7.5 B) 10 C) 40 D) 100	34.
35. Which of the following numbers is the largest? A) $\frac{4}{9}$ B) $\sqrt{\frac{4}{9}}$ C) $(\frac{4}{9})^2$ D) $(\frac{4}{9})^3$	35.
36. In this figure, all angles are right angles. What is the area of this figure? A) 300 B) 325 C) 350 D) 450	36.
37. What percent of 4 hours is 8 seconds? A) 2% B) $\frac{1}{2}$% C) $\frac{1}{9}$% D) $\frac{1}{18}$%	37.
38. The sum of the squares of three whole numbers is 165. The largest of these squares is A) 100 B) 121 C) 144 D) 160	38.
39. Four typists can type a total of 600 letters in 3 days. How many letters can two of these typists type in 1 day? A) 90 B) 100 C) 120 D) 150	39.
40. The sum of the first 100 positive whole numbers is 5050. What is the sum of the first 100 positive odd whole numbers? A) 10 000 B) 10 050 C) 10 100 D) 10 150	40.

The end of the contest ✍ **7**

Solutions on Page 53 · Answers on Page 85

1981-82 Annual 7th Grade Contest

Tuesday, February 9, 1982

7

Instructions

- **Time** You will have only *30 minutes* working time for this contest. You might be *unable* to finish all 40 questions in the time allowed.

- **Scores** Please remember that *this is a contest, not a test*—and there is no "passing" or "failing" score. Few students score as high as 30 points (75% correct). Students with half that, 15 points, *should be commended!*

- **Format and Point Value** This is a multiple-choice contest. Every answer is an A, B, C, or D. For each question, write your answer in the *Answers* column to the right of the question. A correct answer is worth 1 point. Unanswered questions get no credit.

Copyright © 1982 by Mathematics Leagues Inc.

Answers

---

1. $111 + 222 + 333 + 444 =$
   A) $1\,000$ B) $1\,010$ C) $1\,110$ D) $101\,010$

1.

---

2. $\frac{1}{4} =$
   A) 0.2 B) 0.25 C) 0.4 D) 0.5

2.

---

3. If a 6-digit positive integer is added to a 6-digit positive integer, the sum could have
   A) 5 digits   B) 7 digits   C) 8 digits   D) 12 digits

3.

---

4. $10^3 + 10^2 + 10^1 + 1 =$
   A) 10^6 B) 40^6 C) $1\,110$ D) $1\,111$

4.

---

5. In a right triangle, the measure of one angle is 55°. The measure of the smallest angle of this triangle is
   A) 1°   B) 25°   C) 35°   D) 90°

5.

---

6. $\frac{1111}{11} =$
   A) 11   B) 100   C) 101   D) 111

6.

---

7. $19.82 - 18.92 =$
   A) 0.1   B) 0.9   C) 1.1   D) 1.9

7.

---

8. 3% of 900 is
   A) 30   B) 27   C) 9   D) 3

8.

---

9. $\sqrt{25} - \sqrt{16} =$
   A) 1   B) 3   C) 9   D) 11

9.

---

10. In the straight-line drawing, find the measure of $\angle AOC$.

    A) 48°   B) 132°   C) 142°   D) 312°

10.

---

11. A 2-pound pizza is cut into 8 slices of equal weight. Find the weight of three slices of the pizza. (1 pound = 16 ounces.)
    A) 3 ounces   B) 6 ounces   C) 8 ounces   D) 12 ounces

11.

---

12. $6\frac{1}{4} - 5\frac{3}{4}$ has the same value as
    A) $\frac{1}{4} - 5\frac{3}{4}$ B) $1\frac{3}{4} - \frac{1}{4}$ C) $1\frac{1}{4} - \frac{3}{4}$ D) $6 - 5$

12.

---

13. The present time is 1 P.M. What time will it be 3600 seconds from now?
    A) 1 A.M.   B) 2 P.M.   C) 3 P.M.   D) 4 P.M.

13.

---

14. $2 + 2 \times 2 - 2 =$
    A) 4   B) 8   C) 16   D) 64

14.

---

15. Find the area of the shaded region of the square.

8

    A) 4   B) 8   C) 16   D) 64

15.

Go on to the next page ⟩
7

16. $\frac{1}{2} + \frac{2}{3} + \frac{3}{4} =$

   A) $\frac{23}{12}$ B) $\frac{6}{9}$ C) $\frac{6}{24}$ D) $\frac{47}{24}$

16.

17. What is the quotient when 5.1 is divided by 0.017?

   A) 30   B) 300   C) 3 000   D) 30 000

17.

18. $(56 \times 71) + (56 \times 29) =$

   A) 5 500   B) 5 580   C) 5 590   D) 5 600

18.

19. Alice had 28 hits in 70 at bats. At that rate, how many hits should she have in 110 times at bat?

   A) 44   B) 48   C) 68   D) 72

19.

20. How many ¼'s are in ½?

   A) ⅛   B) ¼   C) ½   D) 2

20.

21. Two sides of a triangle have lengths of 16 and 18. The length of the third side *cannot* be

   A) 30   B) 17   C) 7   D) 1

21.

22. $2^5 + 4^3 + 5^2 =$

   A) 11^{11} B) 11^{10} C) 11^5 D) 11^2

22.

23. A worker's daily salary is increased from $40 to $50. What is the percent of increase?

   A) 50%   B) 25%   C) 20%   D) 10%

23.

24. $\left(\frac{1}{3} - \frac{1}{4}\right) - \left(\frac{1}{6} - \frac{1}{12}\right) =$

   A) 0   B) $\frac{1}{24}$ C) $\frac{1}{12}$ D) $\frac{1}{6}$

24.

25. $987 \times 654 \times 321 =$

   A) 207 204 858 B) 207 204 859 C) 207 204 861 D) 207 204 862

25.

26. In 30 years, Sue will be 1½ times as old as she is now. How old is she now?

   A) 15   B) 20   C) 45   D) 60

26.

27. On a scale drawing, a line 5 cm long represents a distance of 40 meters. A line 6¾ cm long represents a distance of

   A) 51 meters   B) 54 meters   C) 57 meters   D) 60 meters

27.

28. If 10 men can build a house in 60 days, then 20 men can build the same house in

   A) 30 days   B) 60 days   C) 90 days   D) 120 days

28.

29. The cost of a tire and a jack is $110. If the tire cost $100 more than the jack, how much did the tire cost?

   A) $5   B) $10   C) $100   D) $105

29.

Go on to the next page ⅢⅢ➡ **7**

30.	For a car to make a 20 mile trip at an average rate of 30 miles per hour, it must complete the trip in A) 20 minutes B) 30 minutes C) 40 minutes D) 50 minutes	30.
31.	The measure of the largest angle in a triangle can *never* be A) 59° B) 61° C) 178° D) 179°30′	31.
32.	50% of 50% of 50 is what percent of 50? A) 100% B) 50% C) 25% D) 12.5%	32.
33.	A store buys pens at 8 for 25¢ and sells them at 2 for 15¢. To make a profit of $3.50, the store must sell A) 10 pens B) 40 pens C) 80 pens D) 100 pens	33.
34.	$\dfrac{2^{150}}{2^{50}} =$ A) 3 B) 100 C) 2^3 D) 2^{100}	34.
35.	What is the sum of all the whole numbers factors of 24? A) 24 B) 48 C) 36 D) 60	35.
36.	The second hand of a clock is 5 cm long. In one hour, the tip of the second hand travels a distance of A) $36\,000\,\pi$ cm B) $6\,000\,\pi$ cm C) $3\,600\,\pi$ cm D) $600\,\pi$ cm	36.
37.	Suppose a and b represent numbers. The symbol $\triangle{a}$, drawn any size, means $a + 4$. The symbol $\boxed{b}$, drawn any size, means b^2. Find the value of $\boxed{3}+\triangle{2}-\triangle{4}$. A) 75 B) 35 C) 32 D) 9	37.
38.	A man has a 10 m × 10 m square garden. In the center is a 2 m × 2 m square patch which he cannot use. He divides his usable space into four congruent rectangular patches, each of which measures A) 3 m × 3 m B) 8 m × 3 m C) 4 m × 6 m D) 2 m × 12 m	38.
39.	One skip = 4 hops, and 1 jump = 2 skips. How many hops are there all together in a hop, skip, and a jump? A) 7 B) 8 C) 12 D) 13	39.
40.	*A wise old owl climbed up a tree* *Whose height was exactly ninety plus three.* *Every day the owl went up eighteen.* *Every night the owl came down thirteen.* *If the owl did not pause or stop,* *When did its claws first reach the top?* A) day 16 B) day 17 C) day 18 D) day 19	40.

The end of the contest ✍ **7**

Solutions on Page 57 · Answers on Page 86

1977-78 Annual 8th Grade Contest

Tuesday, February 14, 1978

8

Instructions

- **Time** You will have only *30 minutes* working time for this contest. You might be *unable* to finish all 40 questions in the time allowed.

- **Scores** Please remember that *this is a contest, not a test*—and there is no "passing" or "failing" score. Few students score as high as 30 points (75% correct). Students with half that, 15 points, *should be commended!*

- **Format and Point Value** This is a multiple-choice contest. Every answer is an A, B, C, or D. For each question, write your answer in the *Answers* column to the right of the question. A correct answer is worth 1 point. Unanswered questions get no credit.

1.	32% is the same as			1.
	A) 32	B) $3\frac{1}{8}$	C) $\frac{8}{25}$	D) none of these

2.	217 is divisible by

A) 3   B) 9   C) 11   D) none of these   2.

3. The intersection of the sets {1, 3, 5, 7} and {1, 2, 3} is   3.

    A) {1, 2, 3, 5, 7}   B) {1}   C) ∅   D) none of these

4. An isosceles right triangle has an angle whose measure is   4.

    A) 45°   B) 60°   C) 180°   D) none of these

5. $2^4 \times 5^4 =$ 5.

    A) 320   B) 2 000   C) 10 000   D) none of these

6. What percent of 44 is 55?   6.

    A) 125%   B) 120%   C) 80%   D) 75%

7. The sum of two numbers is 10. Their product is at most   7.

    A) 9   B) 10   C) 25   D) none of these

8. The perimeter of a square is 32. The area of this square is   8.

    A) 16   B) 32   C) 64   D) none of these

9. To the nearest tenth, 7.63 + 9.32 =   9.

    A) 16.9   B) 17.0   C) 17.9   D) none of these

10. Of 1, 11, 21, 31, 41, and 51, how many are primes?   10.

    A) 3   B) 4   C) 5   D) none of these

11. If d is the length of a circle's diameter, the circle's area is   11.

    A) $\frac{\pi d^2}{4}$ B) $\frac{\pi d^2}{2}$ C) πd^2 D) $2\pi d$

12. The smallest prime number greater than 90 is   12.

    A) 91   B) 93   C) 97   D) none of these

13. Every integer is   13.

    A) irrational   B) real   C) positive   D) non-negative

14. $(6 \times 10^4) + (5 \times 10^2) + (3 \times 10^1) =$ 14.

    A) 653   B) 6053   C) 356   D) none of these

15. Of the numbers 2, 3, 4, and 5, which is (are) the only one(s) which satisfy the inequality $3x - 1 < 11$?   15.

    A) 2   B) 2, 3, and 4   C) 5   D) none of these

Go on to the next page ⫸ **8**

16. When $4\frac{1}{6}$ is divided by $1\frac{2}{3}$, the quotient is

   A) $2\frac{1}{2}$ B) $\frac{2}{5}$ C) $2\frac{1}{5}$ D) none of these

17. The number 5 is the *only* solution to

   I. $x + 15 = 20$ II. $5x \neq 14$

   A) I, not II   B) II, not I   C) I and II   D) none of these

18. $8 \div 2 \times 4 =$

   A) 64   B) 16   C) 4   D) 1

19. The perfect squares, 1, 4, 9, 16, 25, . . . , are closed under
   A) addition   B) multiplication
   C) square-rooting   D) none of these

20. In the base six numeral 3254, the digit 2 represents the number
   A) 36   B) 72   C) 200   D) 216

21. If $a < 10$ and $b < 5$, it *must* be true that
   A) $a > b$ B) $a - b = 5$ C) $a = 2b$ D) $a + b < 20$

22. If p is the smallest prime factor of 511, then
   A) $18 \leq p \leq 23$ B) $10 \leq p \leq 17$ C) $3 \leq p \leq 9$ D) none of these

23. Find the ratio of 9.6 to 8.
   A) 6:5   B) 12:1   C) 1:12   D) none of these

24. If $a \, \S \, b$ means $\frac{a+b}{a \times b}$, find the value of $5 \, \S \, (3 \, \S \, 4)$.

   A) $1\frac{22}{35}$ B) $2\frac{11}{12}$ C) $5\frac{7}{12}$ D) none of these

25. An example of a *false* inequality is
   A) $\frac{2}{9} > \frac{1}{5}$ B) $\frac{5}{7} < \frac{8}{9}$ C) $\frac{2}{7} > \frac{1}{4}$ D) none of these

26. The number 56 is $87\frac{1}{2}\%$ of

   A) 35   B) 49   C) 64   D) none of these

27. In a right triangle, if the lengths of the legs are 10 and 24, the length of the hypotenuse is
   A) 17   B) 26   C) 34   D) 38

28. If N is an even number, which of the following is *always* odd?
   A) $\frac{N}{2} + 1$ B) $\frac{N}{2} + 2$ C) $\frac{N}{2} + 3$ D) none of these

29. If A and B are sets whose union is B, then it *must* be true that
   A) A is a subset of B B) $A = \varnothing$
   C) $A = B$ D) none of these

Go on to the next page ⫸ **8**

30. The difference between a 2-digit number and the number with
    its digits reversed is *always* divisible by

    A) 2   B) 4   C) 6   D) none of these | 30.

31. If $\frac{1}{3}$ of a number is N, then $\frac{5}{6}$ of the number is | 31.

    A) 1.2N B) 2.5N C) 3N D) none of these

32. When expressed as a percent, $0.03\frac{1}{3}$ becomes | 32.

    A) $33\frac{1}{3}\%$ B) $3\frac{1}{3}\%$ C) $0.03\frac{1}{3}\%$ D) none of these

33. The number 124150.5225 is the square of a number which has
    _?_ non-zero digits to the right of its decimal point. | 33.

    A) 2   B) 3   C) 4   D) 5

34. If a girl with an allowance of \$$X$ spends \$$Y$, the fractional part
    of her allowance that she did *not* spend is | 34.

    A) $\frac{X-Y}{X}$ B) $X - Y$ C) $\frac{Y}{X}$ D) none of these

35. A man spent two-thirds of his money and misplaced two-thirds
    of the remainder, leaving him with \$18. With how much money
    did he start? | 35.

    A) \$42   B) \$50   C) \$81   D) none of these

36. If 88 feet per second is the same as 60 miles per hour (mph), a
    plane flying at a speed of 1100 feet per second is traveling at | 36.

    A) 750 mph   B) 740 mph   C) 730 mph   D) none of these

37. An example of numbers written in *increasing* order is | 37.

    A) $\frac{11}{15}, \frac{13}{19}, \frac{13}{23}$ B) $\frac{13}{23}, \frac{13}{19}, \frac{11}{15}$ C) $\frac{13}{23}, \frac{11}{15}, \frac{13}{19}$ D) none of these

38. If m and n are positive two-digit numbers, then, of the
    following fractions, the one with the largest value is | 38.

    A) $\frac{n}{m}$ B) $\frac{n+1}{m-1}$ C) $\frac{n-1}{m}$ D) $\frac{n}{m+1}$

39. If $3N = 5$, then $1 =$ | 39.

    A) $\frac{5}{3}$ B) $\frac{3N}{5}$ C) 0.6   D) none of these

40. At the rate of 4 pens for C¢, how many pens can I buy for 40¢? | 40.

    A) 10C B) $\frac{10}{C}$ C) $\frac{160}{C}$ D) none of these

The end of the contest **8**

Solutions on Page 61 · Answers on Page 87

1978-79 Annual 8th Grade Contest

Tuesday, February 13, 1979

8

Instructions

- **Time** You will have only *30 minutes* working time for this contest. You might be *unable* to finish all 40 questions in the time allowed.

- **Scores** Please remember that *this is a contest, not a test*—and there is no "passing" or "failing" score. Few students score as high as 30 points (75% correct). Students with half that, 15 points, *should be commended!*

- **Format and Point Value** This is a multiple-choice contest. Every answer is an A, B, C, or D. For each question, write your answer in the *Answers* column to the right of the question. A correct answer is worth 1 point. Unanswered questions get no credit.

Copyright © 1979 by Mathematics Leagues Inc.

1. $1.23 + 0.046 =$ A) 1.2346 B) 1.276 C) 1.69 D) 5.83	1.
2. Today is Tuesday. What day of the week was it 365 days ago? A) Sunday B) Monday C) Tuesday D) Wednesday	2.
3. $\frac{11}{12} - \frac{2}{3} =$ A) $\frac{1}{4}$ B) $\frac{9}{12}$ C) 1 D) $\frac{9}{4}$	3.
4. In a right triangle, if one acute angle has a measure of 35°, the other acute angle has a measure of A) 55° B) 65° C) 90° D) 145°	4.
5. $(-8) - (-13) =$ A) -21 B) -5 C) 5 D) 21	5.
6. Find the remainder when $7\,000\,000\,000\,002$ is divided by 9. A) 0 B) 1 C) 2 D) 8	6.
7. $(2.1)^2 - (0.1)^2 =$ A) 4.4 B) 4.1 C) 4.0 D) 3.9	7.
8. Of the following fractions, which is 50% greater than $\frac{3}{7}$? A) $\frac{4}{7}$ B) $\frac{5}{7}$ C) $\frac{7}{10}$ D) $\frac{9}{14}$	8.
9. When $\frac{8}{9}$ is divided by $\frac{4}{3}$, the result is A) $\frac{32}{27}$ B) $\frac{2}{3}$ C) $\frac{2}{27}$ D) 6	9.
10. If $280 = N$, then $350 =$ A) $\frac{N}{4}$ B) $\frac{4N}{5}$ C) $\frac{4N}{3}$ D) $\frac{5N}{4}$	10.
11. Find the average of the 1000 whole numbers from 1 to 1000 inclusive. A) 499.5 B) 500.0 C) 500.5 D) 501.0	11.
12. Find the ratio of 15 centimeters to 3 meters. A) 1:20 B) 1:5 C) 5:1 D) 20:1	12.
13. If $a = 3$ and $b = -4$, then $\frac{2a - b}{a + b} =$ A) -10 B) -2 C) 2 D) $1\frac{3}{7}$	13.
14. If the area of a square is 100, its perimeter is A) 10 B) 25 C) 40 D) 400	14.
15. $10 + 20 \div 2 + 3 =$ A) 6 B) 14 C) 18 D) 23	15.

Go on to the next page ▐▐▐➡ **8**

16. If $N = 6 + 4 + 3 + 1 + \frac{1}{3}N$, then the value of N is

    A) 12   B) 15   C) 18   D) 21

    16.

17. A tennis player uses up 800 calories every hour. In 1 hour and 15 minutes, how many calories does this player use?

    A) 900   B) 1000   C) 1100   D) 1200

    17.

18. If $3a = 5b$, then $a:b =$

    A) 3:5   B) 3:8   C) 5:3   D) 8:3

    18.

19. The sum of the first n positive odd integers is 64. Find n.

    A) 4   B) 6   C) 8   D) 16

    19.

20. The square root of $10 \times 15 \times 24$ is

    A) 60   B) 80   C) 800   D) 6000

    20.

21. If $3x - 6y = 8$, then $x - 2y =$

    A) 4   B) 3   C) $2\frac{2}{3}$ D) 5

    21.

22. Find the value of $(-1)^{1979}$.

    A) -1 B) 1   C) 1979   D) -1979

    22.

23. The length of a rectangle is increased by 20% and its width is decreased by 10%. This increases the area by

    A) 2%   B) 8%   C) 10%   D) 20%

    23.

24. The expression $\dfrac{\frac{1}{2} + \frac{1}{3}}{\frac{1}{2} - \frac{1}{3}}$ is equivalent to

    A) $\frac{1}{6}$ B) 1   C) $\frac{5}{6}$ D) 5

    24.

25. If N is an even integer, then __?__ *must* be an odd integer.

    A) $\frac{1}{2}N$ B) $\frac{1}{2}N + 1$ C) $3N$ D) $3N + 3$

    25.

26. The sum of the repeating decimals $0.\overline{666}$ and $0.\overline{333}$ is

    A) 0.9   B) 99%   C) $\frac{9999}{10000}$ D) 1

    26.

27. When a 3-digit integer is multiplied by a 3-digit integer, the product *may* have

    A) 3 digits   B) 4 digits   C) 6 digits   D) 9 digits

    27.

28. $\frac{1}{9}$ is the square root of

    A) $\frac{1}{3}$ B) $\frac{2}{9}$ C) $\frac{1}{18}$ D) $\frac{1}{81}$

    28.

29. Find the tens' digit in the following product:
    $4 \times 5 \times 6 \times 7 \times 8 \times 9 \times 10 \times 11 \times 12 \times 13 \times 14$.

    A) 0   B) 2   C) 4   D) 8

    29.

Go on to the next page ⫸ **8**

27

30. A girl walks $\frac{3}{4}$ of the way home in 18 minutes. At the same rate, she can walk the rest of the way home in A) $4\frac{1}{2}$ minutes B) 6 minutes C) 9 minutes D) 24 minutes	30.
31. The radius of a circle is 2. When the radius is doubled, by how much is the area increased? A) 16π B) 12π C) 8π D) 4π	31.
32. If $\uparrow N\uparrow = N^2 + 1$ and $\S N\S = \frac{1}{N}$, then $\S(3 + \uparrow 2\uparrow)\S =$ A) $\frac{1}{8}$ B) $\frac{8}{15}$ C) $\frac{7}{12}$ D) $\frac{16}{3}$	32.
33. If $a > 0$ and $b < 0$, which of the following *must* be true? A) $-a < b$ B) $a < -b$ C) $b - a < 0$ D) $ab > 0$	33.
34. In a 36-minute gym period, 24 boys want to play basketball. If only 10 can play at the same time, and each boy plays the same amount of time, how many minutes does each boy play? A) 12 B) 15 C) 18 D) 20	34.
35. The lengths of the sides of a triangle are 6, 8, and 10. The area of this triangle is A) 24 B) 30 C) 40 D) 48	35.
36. If $\begin{vmatrix} a & b \\ c & d \end{vmatrix}$ means $ad - bc$, find the value of $\begin{vmatrix} 5 & 4 \\ 2 & 3 \end{vmatrix}$. A) 2 B) 7 C) 14 D) 22	36.
37. Of 50 people, 38 have brown hair, 29 have brown eyes, and 23 have both brown hair and brown eyes. How many have neither brown hair nor brown eyes? A) 6 B) 8 C) 10 D) 12	37.
38. Find the area of the trapezoid at the right. A) 44 B) 48 C) 90 D) 100	38.
39. In a 10-team league, each team plays every other team exactly twice. Find the total number of games played in the league. A) 20 B) 45 C) 90 D) 180	39.
40. If $a \times b \times a = a^3 \P \frac{a}{b}$, then $\P$ really represents the operation A) $\div$ B) $\times$ C) $+$ D) $-$	40.

The end of the contest **8**

Solutions on Page 65 · Answers on Page 88

1979-80 Annual 8th Grade Contest

Tuesday, February 12, 1980

8

Instructions

- **Time** You will have only *30 minutes* working time for this contest. You might be *unable* to finish all 40 questions in the time allowed.

- **Scores** Please remember that *this is a contest, not a test*—and there is no "passing" or "failing" score. Few students score as high as 30 points (75% correct). Students with half that, 15 points, *should be commended!*

- **Format and Point Value** This is a multiple-choice contest. Every answer is an A, B, C, or D. For each question, write your answer in the *Answers* column to the right of the question. A correct answer is worth 1 point. Unanswered questions get no credit.

1. $5\frac{1}{2} - 2\frac{3}{4} =$ A) $2\frac{3}{4}$ B) $3\frac{1}{4}$ C) $3\frac{1}{2}$ D) $3\frac{3}{4}$	1.
2. Which is nearest in value to 6? A) 5.985 B) 6.005 C) 6.01 D) 6.1	2.
3. The reciprocal of the reciprocal of $1\frac{1}{2}$ is A) $1\frac{1}{2}$ B) $\frac{3}{4}$ C) $\frac{2}{3}$ D) $\frac{1}{2}$	3.
4. How many of the small cubical blocks were needed to construct the rectangular solid pictured? A) 47 B) 48 C) 60 D) 94	4.
5. Last June, it rained 10% of the days. Last June it rained on A) 10 days B) 6 days C) 3 days D) no days	5.
6. $0.40 =$ A) $\frac{1}{25}$ B) $\frac{1}{4}$ C) $\frac{1}{40}$ D) $\frac{2}{5}$	6.
7. The number of different positive two-digit whole numbers is A) 90 B) 91 C) 99 D) 89	7.
8. $\frac{6}{7} =$ A) $\frac{6-2}{7-2}$ B) $\frac{6 \times 6}{7 \times 7}$ C) $\frac{6+2}{7+2}$ D) $\frac{6 \times 2}{7 \times 2}$	8.
9. $(-\frac{1}{2}) \times (-\frac{2}{3}) \times (-\frac{3}{4}) \times (-\frac{4}{5}) =$ A) $\frac{1}{5}$ B) $\frac{1}{2}$ C) $-\frac{1}{2}$ D) $-\frac{1}{5}$	9.
10. If today is Tuesday, May 6, this year July 4 will fall on a A) Sunday B) Monday C) Thursday D) Friday	10.
11. In the *subtraction* problem shown at the right, the two ?'s represent missing digits. The *sum* of these two missing digits is ?1? − 563 847 A) 7 B) 8 C) 9 D) 10	11. 847
12. $2 + 6 \times 6 - 3 \times 2 + 1 =$ A) 29 B) 33 C) 39 D) 91	12.
13. A string in the shape of a 2×8 rectangle can be shaped into a square whose side is A) 5 B) 4 C) 16 D) 20	13.
14. What percent of 39 is 52? A) 66⅔ B) 75% C) 120% D) 133⅓%	14.

Go on to the next page ⏵ **8**

15. $(2^2)^2 =$

    A) 6   B) 8   C) 16   D) 64

  15.

16. A triangle can have sides whose lengths are 9 cm, 16 cm, and

    A) 7 cm   B) 8 cm   C) 25 cm   D) 26 cm

  16.

17. Which is largest?

    A) $5+6+7$ B) $5\times6\times7$ C) $\sqrt{5}+\sqrt{6}+\sqrt{7}$ D) $5^2+6^2+7^2$

  17.

18. If $x + 2 = y$ and $y + 1 = 5$, then $x =$

    A) 1   B) 2   C) 3   D) 4

  18.

19. For which replacement of ♦ will 5470126♦3 be divisible by 9?

    A) 0   B) 3   C) 6   D) 8

  19.

20. $1.6 + 0.16 + 0.016 =$

    A) 1.616   B) 1.666   C) 1.676   D) 1.776

  20.

21. Al calls every 3 days, Lee every 4 days, and Pat every 6 days. Once in every _?_ days, all three will call on the same day.

    A) 9   B) 12   C) 13   D) 15

  21.

22. $(-1)+(-1)\times(-1)\div(-1) =$

    A) -2 B) -1 C) 0   D) 1

  22.

23. If $e = mc^2$, then $\dfrac{e^2}{m^2c^4} =$

    A) e^2 B) 2   C) 1   D) ½

  23.

24. Find the missing number: 22.5:225 = _?_ :22.5

    A) 0.0225   B) 0.225   C) 2.25   D) 225

  24.

25. The figure at the right consists of five squares of the same size. The area of the figure is 180. The perimeter of the figure is

    A) 36   B) 45   C) 72   D) 120

  25.

26. If two consecutive odd numbers are both primes, they are called *twin primes*. One example of a pair of *twin primes* is

    A) 19 and 21   B) 39 and 41   C) 49 and 51   D) 59 and 61

  26.

27. $\dfrac{1}{0.1} + \dfrac{2}{0.2} + \dfrac{3}{0.3} + \dfrac{4}{0.4} =$

    A) 40   B) 10   C) 0.4   D) 0.1

  27.

28. The sum of the first n odd numbers is n^2. The sum of the first 30 odd numbers is

    A) 60   B) 90   C) 300   D) 900

  28.

29. On a reading test, a group of 20 adults averaged 80%, while a group of 30 teenagers averaged 70%. These 50 people averaged

    A) 73%   B) 74%   C) 75%   D) 76%

  29.

Go on to the next page ⫸ **8**

30. $\dfrac{1}{2+\dfrac{3}{4+\dfrac{5}{6}}}$ is equivalent to

    A) $\dfrac{29}{76}$ B) $\dfrac{76}{29}$ C) $\dfrac{20}{29}$ D) $\dfrac{29}{20}$

30.

31. If $x + y = \dfrac{7}{10}$ and $x - y = \dfrac{5}{14}$, then $x^2 - y^2 =$

    A) $(\frac{7}{10})^2-(\frac{5}{14})^2$ B) $(\frac{1}{2})^2$ C) $(\frac{5}{14})^2$ D) $(\frac{7}{10}-\frac{5}{14})^2$

31.

32. A value *between* $\frac{1}{4}$ and $\frac{1}{3}$ is

    A) $\frac{1}{7}$ B) $\frac{4}{13}$ C) $\frac{6}{17}$ D) $\frac{6}{25}$

32.

33. A *Norman Window* is in the shape of a rectangle topped by a semicircle. If the shorter side of the rectangle is 6 and its longer side is 8, the perimeter of the window is

    A) $22 + 18\pi$ B) $22 + 9\pi$ C) $22 + 6\pi$ D) $22 + 3\pi$

33.

34. A shopkeeper makes a profit of 20% of the selling price of an article. The percent profit the shopkeeper makes on the cost is

    A) 20%   B) 25%   C) 40%   D) 80%

34.

35. If $a \divideontimes b$ means $a + b + \dfrac{ab}{10}$, find the value of $[(-5) \divideontimes 2] \divideontimes 4$.

    A) 15.2   B) –13.8   C) –1.6   D) 0

35.

36. Twelve 5-liter cans, filled with syrup, weigh a total of 492 units. Each can, when empty, weighs 3 units. The weight of 1 liter of syrup alone (*without* a can) is most nearly

    A) 5 units   B) 6.5 units   C) 7.5 units   D) 8 units

36.

37. Find the missing number: $\dfrac{20}{30} = \sqrt{\dfrac{20}{?}}$.

    A) 9   B) 30   C) 45   D) 900

37.

38. The length of a radius of a circle is decreased by 10%. This causes the area to be decreased by

    A) 19%   B) 20%   C) 21%   D) 25%

38.

39. A man has 2 pennies, 3 nickels, 1 dime, and 2 quarters. How many different *sums* of money can he make using one or more of these 8 coins?

    A) 8   B) 12   C) 47   D) 77

39.

40. Two cars head towards each other from opposite ends of a highway 450 km long. The speed of the first car is 40 km/h. The speed of the second car is 50 km/h. The cars will meet in

    A) 11.25 hours   B) 10 hours   C) 9 hours   D) 5 hours

40.

The end of the contest **8**

1980-81 Annual 8th Grade Contest

Tuesday, February 10, 1981

8

Instructions

- **Time** You will have only *30 minutes* working time for this contest. You might be *unable* to finish all 40 questions in the time allowed.

- **Scores** Please remember that *this is a contest, not a test*—and there is no "passing" or "failing" score. Few students score as high as 30 points (75% correct). Students with half that, 15 points, *should be commended!*

- **Format and Point Value** This is a multiple-choice contest. Every answer is an A, B, C, or D. For each question, write your answer in the *Answers* column to the right of the question. A correct answer is worth 1 point. Unanswered questions get no credit.

Copyright © 1981 by Mathematics Leagues Inc.

1. Find the units' digit in the product: 2468×8642 A) 2 B) 4 C) 6 D) 8	1.
2. $4\frac{4}{5} =$ A) $\frac{48}{10}$ B) $\frac{24}{10}$ C) $\frac{21}{5}$ D) 4.4	2.
3. $0.77 - 0.7 =$ A) 7.0 B) 0.7 C) 0.07 D) 0.007	3.
4. Find the value of $\sqrt{44}$ to the nearest whole number. A) 8 B) 7 C) 6 D) 5	4.
5. $\frac{1}{6} + \frac{1}{4} + \frac{1}{6} + \frac{1}{4} + \frac{1}{6} =$ A) $\frac{5}{26}$ B) $\frac{5}{24}$ C) $\frac{1}{2}$ D) 1	5.
6. 60 meters of fencing are needed to fence in a square lot. What is the area of the lot? A) 3600 m^2 B) 900 m^2 C) 225 m^2 D) 15 m^2	6.
7. $(0.3)^2 =$ A) 0.9 B) 0.6 C) 0.09 D) 0.06	7.
8. Find the measure of the smaller angle formed by the hands of a clock at 4:00 P.M. A) $110°$ B) $120°$ C) $135°$ D) $150°$	8.
9. $-2 - (-4) =$ A) 2 B) -2 C) 6 D) -6	9.
10. $(4 \times 5 \times 6) \times (\frac{1}{4} \times \frac{1}{5} \times \frac{1}{6}) =$ A) 0 B) 1 C) 3 D) 120	10.
11. Divide 43.416 by 0.06. A) 7236.0 B) 723.6 C) 72.36 D) 7.236	11.
12. The ratio of girls to boys at a school dance was 3 to 2. If there were 30 boys at the dance, how many girls were there? A) 12 B) 18 C) 20 D) 45	12.
13. Find the next number in this sequence: 1, 4, 9, 16, 25, 36, 49, . . . A) 62 B) 63 C) 64 D) 66	13.
14. Which of the following numbers is *not* a factor of 9876? A) 2 B) 3 C) 6 D) 7	14.
15. $0.125 \times 80 =$ A) 0.1 B) 6.4 C) 8 D) 10	15.

Go on to the next page ⮕ **8**

16. Find the missing number: $\frac{?}{10} = \frac{1\frac{1}{2}}{15}$ A) ½ B) 1 C) 1½ D) 2¼	16.
17. The least common multiple of 16 and 24 is A) 4 B) 8 C) 48 D) 384	17.
18. The sum of two positive prime numbers is *always* A) a multiple of 4 B) even C) more than 3 D) odd	18.
19. Of the following numbers, which is largest? A) $\frac{3}{5}$ B) $\frac{2}{3}$ C) 0.67 D) 0.669	19.
20. A car left from Uphere at 9:00 A.M. and arrived at Downthere, 340 km away, at 1:15 P.M. the same day. Find the average speed of the car in kilometers per hour. A) $\frac{340}{7.75}$ B) $\frac{340}{255}$ C) $\frac{340}{415}$ D) $\frac{340}{4.25}$	20.
21. The ratio of the diameters of two circles is 1:4. The ratio of their radii is A) 1:2 B) 1:4 C) 1:8 D) 1:16	21.
22. 25% of 50% of 100 is A) 12½ B) 25 C) 50 D) 75	22.
23. The lengths of the diameters of two concentric circles are 6 and 8. What is the distance between the circles? A) 0 B) 1 C) 2 D) 14	23.
24. $3^3 \times 4^3 =$ A) 12^3 B) 12^6 C) 12^9 D) 5^3	24.
25. An equilateral triangle and a regular hexagon share a common side. The perimeter of the triangle is 20 cm. What is the perimeter of the hexagon? A) 20 cm B) 40 cm C) 60 cm D) 120 cm	25.
26. If $\frac{2}{3}$ ∎ $\frac{3}{2} = 1$, then ∎ really represents the operation A) × B) ÷ C) + D) −	26.
27. If $a = \frac{1}{a}$, then $a^2 =$ A) −1 B) 4 C) 0 D) 1	27.
28. On a certain test, six students scored 75, seven scored 80, eight scored 85, and nine scored 90. What is the overall average of all these students? A) 80 B) 82½ C) 83⅓ D) 84	28.

Go on to the next page ⏭ **8**

35

29. $\sqrt{\frac{1}{4}} + \sqrt{\frac{9}{4}} =$ A) $\sqrt{2}$ B) $\sqrt{\frac{5}{2}}$ C) $\sqrt{4}$ D) $\sqrt{\frac{9}{16}}$	29.
30. $2^{99} + (-2)^{99} =$ A) 0^{99} B) 2^{99} C) 2^{198} D) 4^{99}	30.
31. In parallelogram $PQRS$, $\angle P$ is 4 times $\angle Q$. What is the measure of $\angle P$? A) $110°$ B) $116°$ C) $125°$ D) $144°$	31.
32. The reciprocal of $(\frac{1}{2} + \frac{1}{3})$ is A) 5 B) 2.5 C) 1.2 D) 0.866	32.
33. The area of a right triangle is 30 cm². The length of one leg of the triangle is 5 cm. What is the length of the other leg? A) 6 cm B) 12 cm C) 18 cm D) 24 cm	33.
34. If $n \times 1 \times 2 \times 3 \times 4 = 2 \times 4 \times 6 \times 8$, find the value of n. A) 2 B) 4 C) 8 D) 16	34.
35. A 1 ft × 3 inch × 4 inch rectangular block of ice melts at an average rate of 1 cubic inch per hour. How long does it take for the ice to be totally melted? A) 8 hrs. B) 12 hrs. C) 144 hrs. D) 152 hrs.	35.
36. What percent of 4 hours is 8 seconds? A) 2% B) $\frac{1}{2}$% C) $\frac{1}{9}$% D) $\frac{1}{18}$%	36.
37. Each of a certain type of tire on a 4 wheel car lasts exactly 10 000 miles. How many spare tires of this same variety must be carried so that a trip of 15 000 miles can just be completed (assuming no tires are defective)? A) 1 B) 2 C) 4 D) 6	37.
38. How many of the terms in the sequence 1×12, 2×12, 3×12, $4 \times 12, \ldots$, 15×16, 16×12 are multiples of 16? A) 1 B) 2 C) 4 D) 8	38.
39. The sum of the first 100 positive whole numbers is 5050. What is the sum of the first 100 positive odd whole numbers? A) 10 000 B) 10 050 C) 10 100 D) 10 150	39.
40. The value of d dimes and n nickels is the same as the value of A) $(2d + n)$ nickels B) $(d + 2n)$ nickels C) $(10d + n)$ pennies D) $(d + 5n)$ pennies	40.

The end of the contest ✍ **8**

1981-82 Annual 8th Grade Contest

Tuesday, February 9, 1982

8

Instructions

- **Time** You will have only *30 minutes* working time for this contest. You might be *unable* to finish all 40 questions in the time allowed.

- **Scores** Please remember that *this is a contest, not a test*—and there is no "passing" or "failing" score. Few students score as high as 30 points (75% correct). Students with half that, 15 points, *should be commended!*

- **Format and Point Value** This is a multiple-choice contest. Every answer is an A, B, C, or D. For each question, write your answer in the *Answers* column to the right of the question. A correct answer is worth 1 point. Unanswered questions get no credit.

Copyright © 1982 by Mathematics Leagues Inc.

				Answers
1. $111 \times 999 =$ A) 99 999 B) 109 889 C) 109 989 D) 110 889				1.
2. If a 6-digit positive integer is added to a 6-digit positive integer, the sum could have A) 5 digits B) 7 digits C) 8 digits D) 12 digits				2.
3. $8.8 - 0.88$ A) 0 B) 7.92 C) 8 D) 8.02				3.
4. 5% of $25 is A) $5 B) $2.50 C) $1.25 D) 50¢				4.
5. $\frac{3}{4} =$ A) 0.3 B) 0.6 C) 0.75 D) 0.8				5.
6. The measure of one base angle in an isosceles triangle is 20°. The measure of the largest angle in the triangle is A) 20° B) 90° C) 140° D) 160°				6.
7. 49 divided by 0.7 equals A) 7 B) 10 C) 70 D) 140				7.
8. $(-1) + 2 + (-3) + 4 + (-5) + 6 + (-7) + 8 + (-9) + 10 =$ A) –3 B) 0 C) 4 D) 5				8.
9. Round to the nearest hundredth: 0.03456 A) 0.03 B) 0.04 C) 0.034 D) 0.035				9.
10. The present time is 9 A.M. What time will it be 3600 seconds from now? A) 10 A.M. B) 11 A.M. C) 1 P.M. D) 2 P.M.				10.
11. $(87 \times 96) - (85 \times 96) =$ A) 2 B) 182 C) 192 D) 202				11.
12. $4\frac{1}{6} \times 1\frac{4}{5} =$ A) $4\frac{2}{15}$ B) $5\frac{29}{30}$ C) $7\frac{1}{6}$ D) $7\frac{1}{2}$				12.
13. $2 + 2 \times 2 - 2 =$ A) 0 B) 2 C) 4 D) 6				13.
14. A 2-pound pizza is cut into 8 slices of equal weight. Find the weight of three slices of the pizza. (1 pound = 16 ounces.) A) 3 ounces B) 6 ounces C) 8 ounces D) 12 ounces				14.
15. $87\frac{1}{2}\% =$ A) $\frac{1}{6}$ B) $\frac{7}{8}$ C) $\frac{2}{3}$ D) $\frac{5}{9}$				15.

Go on to the next page ⫸ **8**

16. $\dfrac{20 \times 30 \times 40 \times 50}{2 \times 3 \times 4 \times 5}$

    A) 10   B) 40   C) 1 000   D) 10 000   16.

17. $\dfrac{1}{3} - \dfrac{1}{2} =$

    A) $-\dfrac{1}{6}$ B) $\dfrac{1}{6}$ C) $-\dfrac{5}{6}$ D) $\dfrac{5}{6}$ 17.

18. The area of a square whose perimeter is 2 is   18.

    A) ¼   B) ½   C) 1   D) $\sqrt{2}$

19. $123 \times 456 \times 789 =$ 19.

    A) 44 253 429   B) 44 253 431   C) 44 253 432   D) 44 253 433

20. On a scale drawing, a line 5 cm long represents a distance of   20.
    40 meters. A line 6¾ cm long represents a distance of

    A) 51 meters   B) 54 meters   C) 57 meters   D) 60 meters

21. $5^6 \times 2^6 =$ 21.

    A) 1 000 000   B) 10^{12} C) 7^6 D) 10 000 000

22. If $p - 2$, p, and $p + 2$ are all primes, the *only* possible value of   22.
    p is

    A) 3   B) 5   C) 59   D) 89

23. $\dfrac{1 - 0.50}{1 - 0.25} =$ 23.

    A) ⅛   B) ⅜   C) ⅔   D) 2

24. The measures of a radius of a circle and a side of a square are   24.
    equal. What is the ratio of the area of the circle to the area of
    the square?

    A) 1:1   B) 2π:1   C) π:1   D) 1:π

25. $\sqrt{3^2 + 4^2 + 12^2}$ 25.

    A) 13   B) 19   C) 84   D) 169

26. 1% of 1% of some number is 1. The number is   26.

    A) 100   B) 1 000   C) 10 000   D) 100 000

27. The measure of the smallest angle in a triangle can *never* be   27.

    A) ½°   B) 10°   C) 45°   D) 61°

28. Each angle of a regular hexagon has a measure of   28.

    A) 60°   B) 120°   C) 90°   D) 30°

29. In 30 years, Sue will be 1½ times as old as she is now. How   29.
    old is she now?

    A) 15   B) 20   C) 45   D) 60

30. The cost of a tire and a jack is $110. If the tire cost $100 more   30.
    than the jack, how much did the jack cost?

    A) $5   B) $10   C) $100   D) $105

Go on to the next page ⇒ **8**

31. There are two numbers whose sum is 30 and whose product is 221. These numbers differ by A) 4 B) 3 C) 2 D) 1	31.
32. $\dfrac{3^{200}}{3^{50}} =$ A) 4 B) 150 C) 3^4 D) 3^{150}	32.
33. One liter of paint is needed to cover all 6 sides of a cubical block. How many liters will be needed to cover all 6 sides of a second cubical block whose edge is twice as long as an edge of the first block? A) 2 B) 4 C) 6 D) 8	33.
34. The second hand of a clock is 5 cm long. In one hour, the tip of the second hand travels a distance of A) $600\,\pi$ cm B) $3600\,\pi$ cm C) $6000\,\pi$ cm D) $36000\,\pi$ cm	34.
35. One skip = 4 hops, and 1 jump = 2 skips. How many hops are there all together in a hop, skip, and a jump? A) 7 B) 8 C) 12 D) 13	35.
36. There is a pair of whole numbers a and b, each greater than 1 and less than 10, for which $a^b = b^a + 1$. Find the value of $(a + b)^2$. A) 9 B) 25 C) 36 D) 49	36.
37. A dog weighs $\frac{4}{5}$ of its weight plus 40 pounds. What is the dog's weight? A) 48 pounds B) 72 pounds C) 160 pounds D) 200 pounds	37.
38. A man has a 10 m × 10 m square garden. In the center is a 2 m × 2 m square patch which he cannot use. He divides his usable space into four congruent rectangular patches, each of which measures A) 3 m × 3 m B) 8 m × 3 m C) 4 m × 6 m D) 2 m × 12 m	38.
39. *A wise old owl climbed up a tree* *Whose height was exactly ninety plus three.* *Every day the owl went up eighteen.* *Every night the owl came down thirteen.* *If the owl did not pause or stop,* *When did its claws first reach the top?* A) day 16 B) day 17 C) day 18 D) day 19	39.
40. A man travels a distance of 20 miles at 60 miles per hour and then returns over the same route at 40 miles per hour. Find his average rate for the round trip in miles per hour. A) 50 B) 48 C) 47 D) 46	40.

The end of the contest ✍ **8**

Solutions on Page 77 · Answers on Page 91

Detailed Solutions

●●●●●●●●●●●●●●●●●●

1977-78 through 1981-82

Solutions

1977-78 Annual 7th Grade Contest

Tuesday, February 14, 1978

7

Contest Information

- **Solutions** Turn the page for detailed contest solutions (written in the question boxes) and letter answers (written in the *Answers* column to the right of each question).

- **Scores** Please remember that *this is a contest, not a test*—and there is no "passing" or "failing" score. Few students score as high as 30 points (75% correct). Students with half that, 15 points, *should be commended!*

- **Answers & Rating Scale** Turn to page 82 for the letter answers to each question and the rating scale for this contest.

1. The product of these digits is 0 since one factor is 0. A) 5040 B) 40320 C) 362880 D) none of these	1. D
2. Since the hundredths' digit is less than 5, round down to 8.8. A) 8.85 B) 8.8 C) 8.9 D) none of these	2. B
3. The set of common elements is {1, 3}, so choice D is correct. A) {1,2,3,5,7} B) {1} C) ∅ D) none of these	3. D
4. $\frac{0.42}{0.014} = \frac{0.420}{0.014} = \frac{420}{14} = 420 \div 14 = 30.$ A) 0.03 B) 0.3 C) 3 D) 30	4. D
5. $3141 \times 243 = 763263$, so ? = 6. A) 6 B) 8 C) 9 D) none of these	5. A
6. 55/44 = 5/4 = (5×25)/(4×25) = 125/100 = 125%. A) 125% B) 120% C) 80% D) 75%	6. A
7. If the sum of two numbers is 10, their product is at most 5×5. A) 9 B) 10 C) 25 D) none of these	7. C
8. The perimeter is 32, so each side is 8 and the area is 8×8 = 64. A) 16 B) 32 C) 64 D) none of these	8. C

9. Order makes no difference in both addition & multiplication.
   I. Addition   II. Multiplication
   A) only I   B) only II   C) I and II   D) none of these
	9.
	C

10. 11, 31, and 41 are prime numbers. A) 3 B) 4 C) 5 D) none of these	10. A
11. A circle's area is $\pi r^2 = \pi(d/2)^2 = \pi d^2/4.$ A) $\frac{\pi d^2}{4}$ B) $\frac{\pi d^2}{2}$ C) πd^2 D) $2\pi d$	11. A
12. $91 = 7 \times 13$ and $93 = 3 \times 31$, but 97 is prime. A) 91 B) 93 C) 97 D) none of these	12. C
13. 12/80 = 3/20 = 15/100 = 15%. A) 30% B) 20% C) 15% D) none of these	13. C
14. $(6 \times 10^4) + (5 \times 10^2) + (3 \times 10^1) = 60000 + 500 + 30 = 60530.$ A) 653 B) 6053 C) 356 D) none of these	14. D
15. The only set with exactly one subset is the empty set. A) 0 B) 1 C) 2 D) none of these	15. A

Go on to the next page ⫸ **7**

42

16. $4\frac{1}{6} \div 1\frac{2}{3} = \frac{25}{6} \div \frac{5}{3} = \frac{25}{6} \times \frac{3}{5} = \frac{5}{2} = 2\frac{1}{2}.$

A) $2\frac{1}{2}$ B) $\frac{2}{5}$ C) $2\frac{1}{5}$ D) none of these

16.

A

17. None of the choices is of the form $a(b + c) = (a \times b) + (a \times c)$.

A) $3(4 \times 5) = (3 \times 4)(3 \times 5)$ B) $3(4 + 5) = 3(5 + 4)$
C) $3(4 \times 5) = 3 \times 4 \times 5$ D) none of these

17.

D

18. $8 \div 2 \times 4 = 4 \times 4 = 16.$

A) 64   B) 16   C) 4   D) 1

18.

B

19. In a class of 30, 12 are boys. If 6 more boys are admitted, there are 18 boys in a class of 36; $18/36 = 1/2$, so choice B is correct.

A) $\frac{1}{3}$ B) $\frac{1}{2}$ C) $\frac{2}{5}$ D) none of these

19.

B

20. From right to left, place values are 1, 6^1, 6^2, and 6^3; $2 \times 36 = 72.$

A) 36   B) 72   C) 200   D) 216

20.

B

21. $4 + 3 \times 5 - 2 = 4 + 15 - 2 = 19 - 2 = 17.$

A) 13   B) 21   C) 33   D) none of these

21.

D

22. In all, she won 12 out of 18 matches. Since $12/18 = 2/3 =$ 66⅔%, choice C is correct.

A) $\frac{2}{3}\%$ B) 50%   C) $66\frac{2}{3}\%$ D) none of these

22.

C

23. $9.6{:}8 = 96{:}80 = 48{:}40 = 24{:}20 = 12{:}10 = 6{:}5.$

A) 6:5   B) 12:1   C) 1:12   D) none of these

23.

A

24. Since 42 is divisible by both 14 and 21, choice C is correct.

A) 7   B) $14 \times 21 \times 42$ C) 42   D) none of these

24.

C

25. Dividing by $\frac{1}{2}$ is the same as multiplying by 2; the number has been multiplied by 3 and then 2. Equivalently, multiply by 6.

A) $\frac{3}{2}$ B) $\frac{2}{3}$ C) 6   D) none of these

25.

C

26. $87\frac{1}{2}\% = 7/8$; 56 is 7/8 of 64.

A) 35   B) 49   C) 64   D) none of these

26.

C

27. If the lengths of the legs are 10 and 24, the length of the hypotenuse is the square root of $10^2 + 24^2 = 26.$

A) 17   B) 26   C) 34   D) 38

27.

B

28. All are even since each remainder is 0 when divided by 2.

A) 0   B) 1   C) 2   D) 3

28.

D

29. If the union is B, A must have only elements that are also in B.

A) A is a subset of B B) $A = \emptyset$
C) $A = B$ D) none of these

29.

A

Go on to the next page ⫸ **7**

30. Try a few pairs of numbers like 76 and 67. The difference is *always* divisible by 9.

     A) 2   B) 4   C) 6   D) none of these

30. D

31. $11.70 ÷ $0.65 = 18, so I can buy 18 × 3 = 54 grams for 65¢.

     A) 18 grams   B) 54 grams   C) 62 grams   D) none of these

31. B

32. When expressed as a percent, $0.03\frac{1}{3} = (0.03\frac{1}{3} \times 100)\% = 3\frac{1}{3}\%$.

     A) $33\frac{1}{3}\%$ B) $3\frac{1}{3}\%$ C) $0.03\frac{1}{3}\%$ D) none of these

32. B

33. Square a number with 2 decimal places. The result has 4 decimal places. Reverse the process for this problem.

     A) 2   B) 3   C) 4   D) 5

33. A

34. A discount of 18% means a cost of 82%; similarly, a discount of 23% means a cost of 77%. Since multiplication is commutative, it makes no difference if a number is multiplied first by 82% and then by 77% *or* if the percents are multiplied in the reverse order. The final price is the same either way.

     A) cheaper   B) more expensive
     C) the same   D) none of these

34. C

35. For each $9 the man began with, he spent $6 and lost $2, leaving him with $1. Since he was left with $18, he began with 9 × $18 = $162.

     A) $42   B) $50   C) $81   D) none of these

35. D

36. Since 19 suitcases cost $225, 57 suitcases cost 3 × $225 = $675.

     A) $674.88   B) $675.45   C) $684.00   D) none of these

36. D

37. $a/b < c/d$ if $a \times d < b \times c$; thus, choice B is correct.

     A) $\frac{11}{15}, \frac{13}{19}, \frac{13}{23}$ B) $\frac{13}{23}, \frac{13}{19}, \frac{11}{15}$ C) $\frac{13}{23}, \frac{11}{15}, \frac{13}{19}$ D) none of these

37. B

38. 1 gram:12¢ = 1¾:21¢ = 3:36¢ = 6:72¢; so choice A is cheapest.

     A) $1\frac{3}{4}$ grams for 19¢   B) $2\frac{5}{6}$ grams for 39¢

     C) $5\frac{3}{7}$ grams for 79¢   D) 1 gram for 12¢

38. A

39. $2 + \dfrac{1}{3 + \frac{1}{4}} = 2 + \dfrac{1}{\frac{13}{4}} = 2 + 1 \div \frac{13}{4} = 2 + 1 \times \frac{4}{13} = 2\frac{4}{13}$.

     A) $3\frac{1}{4}$ B) $2\frac{4}{13}$ C) $2\frac{1}{13}$ D) none of these

39. B

40. $1.66 = 62¢ + $1.04 = 62¢ + 13 × 8¢; so there are 5 + 13 = 18 letters in the name.

     A) 13   B) 18   C) 20   D) none of these

40. B

The end of the contest 👉 **7**

Solutions

1978-79 Annual 7th Grade Contest

Tuesday, February 13, 1979

7

Contest Information

- **Solutions** Turn the page for detailed contest solutions (written in the question boxes) and letter answers (written in the *Answers* column to the right of each question).

- **Scores** Please remember that *this is a contest, not a test*—and there is no "passing" or "failing" score. Few students score as high as 30 points (75% correct). Students with half that, 15 points, *should be commended!*

- **Answers & Rating Scale** Turn to page 83 for the letter answers to each question and the rating scale for this contest.

1. 41.7 − 32.8 = 41.7 − 32.7 − 0.1 = 9.0 − 0.1 = 8.9. A) 74.5 B) 9.1 C) 11.1 D) 8.9	1. D
2. 3 of 16 squares are shaded; 3/16 = 18¾%. A) 18% B) $\frac{3}{16}$% C) $18\frac{3}{4}$% D) 3%	2. C
3. When ? is divided by 3, the quotient is 6 and the remainder is 0. Therefore, ? = 3×6 + 0 = 18. A) 18 B) 9 C) 3 D) 2	3. A
4. 5% of 2400 = 5/100×2400 = 5×24 = 120. A) 1200 B) 120 C) 24 D) 12	4. B
5. $\frac{8}{9}\div\frac{4}{3} = \frac{8}{9}\times\frac{3}{4} = \frac{24}{36} = \frac{2}{3}$. A) $\frac{32}{27}$ B) $\frac{2}{3}$ C) $\frac{2}{27}$ D) 6	5. B
6. In a right triangle, if one acute angle has a measure of 48°, the other acute angle has a measure of 90° − 48° = 42°. A) 42° B) 52° C) 90° D) 132°	6. A
7. 0.2×0.3 = 0.06, so choice B is correct. A) 0.006 B) 0.06 C) 0.6 D) 6	7. B
8. The sum of the digits of 2 000 000 000 001 is 3, so remainder is 0. A) 0 B) 1 C) 2 D) 4	8. A
9. $\frac{0.015}{0.03} = \frac{0.015}{0.030} = \frac{15}{30} = \frac{1}{2} = 0.5$. A) 0.005 B) 0.05 C) 0.5 D) 5	9. C
10. Pair 1 & 1000, 2 & 999, 3 & 998, . . . , 499 & 502, and 500 & 501. Each pair has an average of 500.5, so choice C is correct. A) 499.5 B) 500.0 C) 500.5 D) 501.0	10. C
11. 15 cm:3 m = 15 cm:300 cm = (15÷5):(300÷5) = 3:60 = 1:20. A) 1:20 B) 1:5 C) 5:1 D) 20:1	11. A
12. The divisors of 12 are 1, 2, 3, 4, 6, & 12. There are six. A) two B) three C) four D) six	12. D
13. 10 + 20 ÷ 2 + 3 = 10 + (20 ÷ 2) + 3 = 10 + 10 + 3 = 23. A) 6 B) 14 C) 18 D) 23	13. D
14. 2.97×4.13 is approximately equal to 3×4 = 12. A) 120 B) 12 C) 1.2 D) 0.12	14. B
15. If the area of a square is 64, each side is 8 and perimeter is 32. A) 256 B) 128 C) 64 D) 32	15. D
16. $\frac{1}{2} + \frac{1}{25} = \frac{25}{50} + \frac{2}{50} = \frac{27}{50} = \frac{54}{100} = 0.54$. A) 0.50 B) 0.52 C) 0.54 D) 0.56	16. C

Go on to the next page ⫸ **7**

17. 120 is smallest choice divisible by 6, 8, 10, and 12. A) 360 B) 240 C) 60 D) 120	17. D
18. A tennis player uses up 800 calories every hour. In 1 hour and 15 minutes, this player uses $1\frac{1}{4} \times 800 = 1000$ calories. A) 900 B) 1000 C) 1100 D) 1200	18. B
19. The only prime number which is divisible by 17 is 17. A) 0 B) 1 C) 2 D) 3	19. B
20. $6/15 = 2/5 = (2/5 \times 100)\% = 40\%$. A) 25% B) 30% C) 40% D) 60%	20. C
21. $2^{10} = 2 \times 2 \times 2 \times 2 \times 2 \times 2 \times 2 \times 2 \times 2 \times 2 = 1024$; this is the largest. A) 2^{10} B) 3^4 C) 4^3 D) 10^2	21. A
22. Of the 90% of students in a math class who got a passing grade, 10% got $B+$ or better. Since 10% of 90% $= 9\%$, 9% of the entire math class received $B+$ or better. A) 7% B) 8% C) 9% D) 10%	22. C
23. 365 days = 52 weeks and 1 day. If today is Tuesday, 52 weeks from today is also Tuesday and 1 day later is Wednesday. A) Monday B) Tuesday C) Wednesday D) Thursday	23. C
24. If two straight lines intersect as shown, then $x° = y° = 40°$ and $x° + y° = 80°$. A) 20° B) 40° C) 80° D) 180°	24. C
25. $\dfrac{\frac{1}{2}+\frac{1}{3}}{\frac{1}{2}-\frac{1}{3}} = \dfrac{\frac{3+2}{6}}{\frac{3-2}{6}} = \dfrac{5}{6} \div \dfrac{1}{6} = \dfrac{5}{6} \times \dfrac{6}{1} = 5$. A) $\frac{1}{6}$ B) 1 C) $\frac{5}{6}$ D) 5	25. D
26. $100 \times 100 = 10\,000$ and $1000 \times 1000 = 1\,000\,000$; the product must have at least 5 digits and must have fewer than 7 digits. A) 3 digits B) 4 digits C) 6 digits D) 9 digits	26. C
27. $2\frac{1}{2} \times 3\frac{3}{4} \times 5\frac{1}{3} = \frac{5}{2} \times \frac{15}{4} \times \frac{16}{3} = \frac{5}{1} \times \frac{5}{1} \times \frac{2}{1} = 50$. A) 50 B) $31\frac{7}{12}$ C) $30\frac{1}{8}$ D) $11\frac{7}{12}$	27. A
28. Since $\frac{1}{4} \times \frac{1}{4} = \frac{1}{16}$, $\frac{1}{4}$ is the square root of $\frac{1}{16}$. A) $\frac{1}{2}$ B) $\frac{1}{4}$ C) $\frac{1}{8}$ D) $\frac{1}{16}$	28. D
29. A girl walks $\frac{3}{4}$ of the way home in 18 minutes. Since $\frac{1}{4} = \frac{1}{3} \times \frac{3}{4}$, she can walk the rest of the way home, $\frac{1}{4}$, in $\frac{1}{3} \times 18 = 6$ mins. A) $4\frac{1}{2}$ minutes B) 6 minutes C) 9 minutes D) 24 minutes	29. B

Go on to the next page ⫸ **7**

30. If the circumferences of two circles are in the ratio 2:3, then their areas are in the ratio $2^2 : 3^2 = 4:9$. A) 2:3 B) 2:5 C) 3:5 D) 4:9	30. D
31. $\frac{1}{9}$ of $3 = \frac{1}{3}$; $\frac{2}{5}$ of $1\frac{2}{3} = \frac{2}{5} \times \frac{5}{3} = \frac{2}{3}$; $\frac{2}{3} - \frac{1}{3} = \frac{1}{3}$. A) $\frac{2}{25}$ B) $\frac{1}{6}$ C) $\frac{1}{3}$ D) $\frac{18}{25}$	31. C
32. She had 8 dimes and 12 nickels and spent 5 dimes and 3 nickels, leaving 3 dimes and 9 nickels. A) 7 B) 9 C) 11 D) 12	32. B
33. Every $\frac{1}{3}$ cup of sugar requires $\frac{1}{2}$ cup of flour. Since 1 cup of sugar = $\frac{3}{3}$ cups, the amount of flour needed is $3 \times \frac{1}{2} = 1\frac{1}{2}$ cups. A) 1 cup B) $1\frac{1}{8}$ cups C) $1\frac{1}{4}$ cups D) $1\frac{1}{2}$ cups	33. D
34. To average 75, the six grades must total $6 \times 75 = 450$. Since the total so far is 384, his next test grade must be $450 - 384 = 66$. A) 66 B) 68 C) 71 D) 75	34. A
35. $3/5 = 0.60$; $5/8 = 0.625$; $2/3 = 0.\overline{66}$; $7/11 = 0.\overline{63}$. Choice C has them listed in increasing size order. A) $\frac{7}{11}, \frac{5}{8}, \frac{3}{5}, \frac{2}{3}$ B) $\frac{3}{5}, \frac{5}{8}, \frac{2}{3}, \frac{7}{11}$ C) $\frac{3}{5}, \frac{5}{8}, \frac{7}{11}, \frac{2}{3}$ D) $\frac{2}{3}, \frac{3}{5}, \frac{5}{8}, \frac{7}{11}$	35. C
36. Jack picks 15 liters of berries in 40 minutes. Jill picks 16 liters of berries in 40 minutes. Working together, they pick 31 liters in 40 minutes. Therefore, in 1 minute they pick 31/40 of a liter. A) $\frac{7}{9}$ B) $\frac{7}{18}$ C) $\frac{8}{19}$ D) $\frac{31}{40}$	36. D
37. Since 10 boys can play for 36 minutes, 360 minutes of play time is available. If 24 boys share this time equally, each boy gets (360 minutes) ÷ 24 = 15 minutes. A) 12 B) 15 C) 18 D) 20	37. B
38. Since $6^2 + 8^2 = 10^2$, the triangle is a right triangle. Using one leg as the base and the other as the height, area = $\frac{1}{2} \times 6 \times 8 = 24$. A) 24 B) 30 C) 40 D) 48	38. A
39. 15 people with brown hair have non-brown eyes, 6 with brown eyes have non-brown hair, and 23 with brown hair have brown eyes. This accounts for 44 people, leaving 6 with neither trait. A) 6 B) 8 C) 10 D) 12	39. A
40. Every team plays 18 games. Each game is played by 2 teams. The number of games is $\frac{1}{2}(18 \times 10) = 90$. A) 20 B) 45 C) 90 D) 180	40. C

The end of the contest 🖎 **7**

Solutions

1979-80 Annual 7th Grade Contest

Tuesday, February 12, 1980

7

Contest Information

- **Solutions** Turn the page for detailed contest solutions (written in the question boxes) and letter answers (written in the *Answers* column to the right of each question).

- **Scores** Please remember that *this is a contest, not a test*—and there is no "passing" or "failing" score. Few students score as high as 30 points (75% correct). Students with half that, 15 points, *should be commended!*

- **Answers & Rating Scale** Turn to page 84 for the letter answers to each question and the rating scale for this contest.

1. $4444 - 444 + 44 - 4 = (4444 - 444) + (44 - 4) = 4000 + 40 = 4040.$ A) 4936 B) 4040 C) 3960 D) 3952	1. B
2. Rewrite 1st 2 choices as 8.100 & 8.010. Choice C is nearest to 8. A) 8.1 B) 8.01 C) 8.005 D) 7.985	2. C
3. $6\frac{3}{4} + 2\frac{1}{2} = 6\frac{3}{4} + 2\frac{2}{4} = 8\frac{5}{4} = 9\frac{1}{4}.$ A) $9\frac{1}{4}$ B) 9 C) $8\frac{3}{4}$ D) $8\frac{1}{4}$	3. A
4. If the measure of one angle of a right triangle is 70°, the smallest angle of the triangle has a measure of $90° - 70° = 20°.$ A) 1° B) 10° C) 15° D) 20°	4. D
5. $\frac{7}{9} = \frac{7 \times 2}{9 \times 2}$, since numerator and denominator are *multiplied* by 2. A) $\frac{7-2}{9-2}$ B) $\frac{7 \times 7}{9 \times 9}$ C) $\frac{7+2}{9+2}$ D) $\frac{7 \times 2}{9 \times 2}$	5. D
6. There are 30 days in June; 10% of $30 = 1/10 \times 30 = 3.$ A) 10 days B) 6 days C) 3 days D) no days	6. C
7. $\frac{-3}{10} \times \frac{-5}{6} = \frac{15}{60} = \frac{1}{4}.$ A) $\frac{1}{4}$ B) $\frac{1}{2}$ C) 2 D) 4	7. A
8. There are 99 such numbers from 1 to 99; from 10 to 99 is 9 fewer. A) 90 B) 91 C) 99 D) 89	8. A
9. $25 + 250 = (25 \times 1) + (25 \times 10) = 25 \times (1 + 10) = 25 \times 11.$ A) 10 B) 11 C) 25 D) 250	9. B
10. $\frac{1+2+3+4+5}{2+4+6+8+10} = \frac{1 \times (1+2+3+4+5)}{2 \times (1+2+3+4+5)} = \frac{1}{2}.$ A) $\frac{1}{32}$ B) $\frac{1}{15}$ C) $\frac{1}{2}$ D) 1	10. C
11. The top number is the sum of 563 and 347. ?1? Since their sum is 910, the missing digits are -563 are 9 and 0 and their sum is $9 + 0 = 9.$ 347 A) 10 B) 9 C) 8 D) 7	11. B
12. $0.1 \times 0.2 \times 0.3 = (0.1 \times 0.2) \times 0.3 = 0.02 \times 0.3 = 0.006.$ A) 0.0006 B) 0.006 C) 0.06 D) 0.6	12. B
13. The area of the square is 2×18 cm^2 = 36 cm^2. Each side of the square is 6 cm and its perimeter is 4×6 cm = 24 cm. A) 18 cm B) 20 cm C) 24 cm D) 36 cm	13. C
14. $0.2 \times 60 = (0.1 \times 2) \times (3 \times 20) = 0.1 \times 3 \times 2 \times 20 = 0.3 \times 40 = 30\%$ of 40. A) 40 B) 50 C) 90 D) 100	14. A
15. $2 + (6 \times 6) - (3 \times 2) + 1 = 2 + 36 - 6 + 1 = 33.$ A) 29 B) 33 C) 39 D) 91	15. B

Go on to the next page ▐▐▐➡ 7

16.	Whole numbers divisors of 36 are 1, 2, 3, 4, 6, 9, 12, 18, & 36.			16. D
	A) 6 B) 7 C) 8 D) 9			

16. Whole numbers divisors of 36 are 1, 2, 3, 4, 6, 9, 12, 18, & 36.
    A) 6   B) 7   C) 8   D) 9

16. D

17. Choice A has smallest numerator and largest denominator.
    A) $\frac{0.2}{5}$ B) $\frac{2}{0.5}$ C) $\frac{0.2}{0.5}$ D) $\frac{0.5}{2}$

17. A

18. The sum of the two smaller sides must be greater than the 3rd.
    A) 7 cm   B) 8 cm   C) 25 cm   D) 26 cm

18. B

19. The units' digit of $1980^2 + 1981^2 + 1982^2$ is $0^2 + 1^2 + 2^2 = 5$.
    A) 3   B) 4   C) 5   D) 6

19. C

20. If the average of four numbers is 20, their sum is $4 \times 20 = 80$.
    The average of these four numbers and 15 is $(80 + 15) \div 5 = 19$.
    A) 17   B) 19   C) 21   D) 23

20. B

21. $567\overline{)567\,567\,567\,567} = 1\,001\,001\,001$, so choice D is correct.
    A) 4   B) 1111   C) 1010101   D) 1 001 001 001

21. D

22. Carole now has 4 times as many tapes as she had last year. She
    has 64 tapes now. Last year, she had $64 \div 4 = 16$ tapes.
    A) 16   B) 32   C) 48   D) 256

22. A

23. $0.0009 = 0.03 \times 0.03$, so choice C is correct.
    A) 0.0003   B) 0.003   C) 0.03   D) 0.3

23. C

24. Since the area of the 5 squares is 180, each has
    an area of $180 \div 5 = 36$. A side of each square is
    6 and the perimeter of the figure is $12 \times 6 = 72$.
    A) 36   B) 45   C) 72   D) 120

24. C

25. $3^3 + 3^3 + 3^3 = 3 \times 27 = 81 = 3^4$.
    A) 9^9 B) 9^3 C) 3^9 D) 3^4

25. D

26. 21, 39, and 51 are *all* divisible by 3. Only choice D has a pair
    of prime numbers which differ by 2.
    A) 19 and 21   B) 39 and 41   C) 49 and 51   D) 59 and 61

26. D

27. $7/9 = 0.\overline{77}$; $5/9 = 0.\overline{55}$, $8/11 = 0.\overline{72}$; $9/12 = 0.75$. A is largest.
    A) $\frac{7}{9}$ B) $\frac{5}{9}$ C) $\frac{8}{11}$ D) $\frac{9}{12}$

27. A

28. Use the Pythagorean Theorem: $34^2 - 16^2 = 1156 - 256 = 900$;
    the ladder reaches $\sqrt{900}$ m $= 30$ m up the wall.
    A) 24   B) 26   C) 28   D) 30

28. D

29. $\frac{4}{40} = 0.10$ & $\frac{5}{40} = 0.125$; $\frac{1}{9} = 0.\overline{11}$ which is closer to $\frac{4}{40}$ than $\frac{5}{40}$.
    A) $\frac{4}{40}$ B) $\frac{5}{40}$ C) $\frac{6}{40}$ D) $\frac{7}{40}$

29. A

Go on to the next page ⟱ **7**

30. The least common multiple of 3, 4, and 6 is 12. Thus, once in every 12 days, all three will call on the same day.

    A) 9   B) 12   C) 13   D) 15

    30. **B**

31. 33.4:334 = (33.4÷10):(334÷10) = 3.34:33.4, so choice C is correct.

    A) 0.0334   B) 0.334   C) 3.34   D) 334

    31. **C**

32. On each $100, the shopkeeper makes $20. Thus, the profit is $20 for a cost of $80. Since 20/80 = 1/4 = 25%, choice B is correct.

    A) 20%   B) 25%   C) 40%   D) 80%

    32. **B**

33. The value of 5! + 5 is $5 \times 4 \times 3 \times 2 \times 1 + 5 = 120 + 5 = 125$.

    A) 10   B) 25   C) 29   D) 125

    33. **D**

34. Powers of 27 (cyclically) end in 7, 9, 3, 1, 7, 9, 3, 1 . . . . .

    A) 1   B) 3   C) 7   D) 9

    34. **B**

35. The perimeter of the window consists of 3 sides of the rectangle plus the circumference of a semi-circle of radius 3. Perimeter $= 8 + 8 + 6 + 3\pi = 22 + 3\pi$.

    A) $22 + 18\pi$ B) $22 + 9\pi$ C) $22 + 6\pi$ D) $22 + 3\pi$

    35. **D**

36. $$\cfrac{1}{2 + \cfrac{3}{4 + \cfrac{5}{6}}} = \cfrac{1}{2 + \cfrac{3}{\frac{29}{6}}} = \cfrac{1}{2 + \frac{18}{29}} = \cfrac{1}{\frac{76}{29}} = \frac{29}{76}.$$

    A) $\frac{29}{20}$ B) $\frac{20}{29}$ C) $\frac{29}{76}$ D) $\frac{76}{29}$

    36. **C**

37. Twelve 5-liter cans, filled with syrup, weigh 492 units. Each can, filled with syrup, weighs $492 \div 12 = 41$ units. The weight of 1 liter of syrup (*without* a can of 3 units) is $(41 - 3) \div 5 = 7.6$ units.

    A) 5 units   B) 6.5 units   C) 7.5 units   D) 8 units

    37. **C**

38. $(9 * 15) * 24 = (\frac{9 + 15}{2}) * 24 = 12 * 24 = \frac{12 + 24}{2} = 18$.

    A) 24   B) 18   C) 16   D) 12

    38. **B**

39. If radius is 10, area is 100π. If radius is decreased 10% to 9, area is 81π. This is a decrease of 19π from 100π or 19%.

    A) 19%   B) 20%   C) 21%   D) 25%

    39. **A**

40. In cents, the attainable sums are 1, 2, 5, 6, 7, 10, 11, 12, 15, 16, 17, . . . , 75, 76, 77. The only *unattainable* sums are those requiring 3 or 4 pennies; there are 30 *unattainable* sums less than 77.

    A) 8   B) 12   C) 47   D) 77

    40. **C**

The end of the contest ✍ **7**

Solutions

1980-81 Annual 7th Grade Contest

Tuesday, February 10, 1981

7

Contest Information

- **Solutions** Turn the page for detailed contest solutions (written in the question boxes) and letter answers (written in the *Answers* column to the right of each question).

- **Scores** Please remember that *this is a contest, not a test*—and there is no "passing" or "failing" score. Few students score as high as 30 points (75% correct). Students with half that, 15 points, *should be commended!*

- **Answers & Rating Scale** Turn to page 85 for the letter answers to each question and the rating scale for this contest.

1. $8642+2468 = (8000+2000)+(600+400)+(40+60)+(2+8) = 11\,110.$
   A) 10000   B) 10010   C) 10110   D) 11110

   1. D

2. $3\frac{3}{5} = 3 + \frac{3}{5} = \frac{30}{10} + \frac{6}{10} = \frac{36}{10}.$
   A) $\frac{36}{10}$ B) $\frac{18}{10}$ C) $\frac{4}{5}$ D) 3.3

   2. A

3. Use the units' digit of each number: $9 \times 3 = 27$, so B is correct.
   A) 9   B) 7   C) 5   D) 3

   3. B

4. $0.66 - 0.6 = 0.66 - 0.60 = 0.06.$
   A) 6.0   B) 0.6   C) 0.06   D) 0.006

   4. C

5. $(1 + 2 + 3 + 4 + 5) + (95 + 96 + 97 + 98 + 99) = 5 \times 100 = 500.$
   A) 100   B) 498   C) 499   D) 500

   5. D

6. Ninety and seven hundredths $= 90 + 0.07 = 90.07.$
   A) 790.0   B) 90.7   C) 90.07   D) 0.97

   6. C

7. The sum of the digits of 87 is a multiple of 3, so $87 = 3 \times 29.$
   A) 107   B) 87   C) 67   D) 47

   7. B

8. 1% of $\$23\,000 = 1/100 \times \$23\,000 = \$23\,000 \div 100 = \$230.$
   A) \$0.023   B) \$23   C) \$230   D) \$2300

   8. C

9. The measure of the complement of $\angle A$ is $25°$. The measure of $\angle A$ is $90° - 25° = 65°.$
   A) $25°$ B) $65°$ C) $75°$ D) $155°$

   9. B

10. $0.03 \times 0.02 = 3/100 \times 2/100 = 6/10\,000 = 0.0006.$
    A) 0.6   B) 0.06   C) 0.006   D) 0.0006

    10. D

11. The common factors of 16 and 24 are 1, 2, 4, & 8; largest is 8.
    A) 4   B) 8   C) 48   D) 384

    11. B

12. $\frac{20 \times 30 \times 40}{2 \times 3 \times 4} = \frac{20}{2} \times \frac{30}{3} \times \frac{40}{4} = 10 \times 10 \times 10 = 1000.$
    A) 1000   B) 300   C) 30   D) 10

    12. A

13. Steve reads 20 pages in 50 minutes, so he reads 10 pages in 25 minutes and 50 pages in $5 \times 25 = 125$ minutes $= 2$ hr 5 min.
    A) 20 min   B) 1 hr 20 min   C) 1 hr 45 min   D) 2 hr 5 min

    13. D

14. Last digit's 0; 2 & 5 are factors. Sum of digits is 12; 3 is a factor.
    A) 7   B) 5   C) 3   D) 2

    14. A

15. 60 meters of fencing are needed to fence in a square lot. Each side is $60 \div 4 = 15$ m. The area of the lot is $15^2 = 225$ m^2.
    A) 3600 m^2 B) 900 m^2 C) 225 m^2 D) 15 m^2

    15. C

16. $43.416 \div 0.06 = 4341.6 \div 6 = 723.6.$
    A) 7.236   B) 72.36   C) 723.6   D) 7236.0

    16. C

Go on to the next page Ⅲ➡ **7**

17. In a school of 300 students, 27 were absent. The percent of absent students is $(27/300) \times 100 = 9/100 \times 100 = 9$.

    A) 9%   B) 27%   C) 81%   D) 91%

    17.

    A

18. $\frac{1}{4}$ of 5 hr 20 min $= \frac{1}{4} \times 320$ min $= 80$ min $= 1$ hr 20 min.

    A) 1 hr 15 min B) 1 hr 20 min C) 1 hr 35 min D) 1 hr 40 min

    18.

    B

19. $1^9 + 1^{10} + 1^{11} = 1 + 1 + 1 = 3 = 3^1$.

    A) 1^{30} B) 3^1 C) 3^{10} D) 3^{30}

    19.

    B

20. The ratio of the diameters is 1:4. If the original diameters were 2 and 8, the radii would be 1 and 4; ratio is *still* 1:4.

    A) 1:2   B) 1:4   C) 1:8   D) 1:16

    20.

    B

21. $0.87\frac{1}{2} + \frac{1}{8} = 0.87\frac{1}{2} + 0.12\frac{1}{2} = 0.875 + 0.125 = 1.000 = 1$.

    A) 1   B) $0.99\frac{1}{2}$ C) $0.95\frac{1}{2}$ D) $0.87\frac{5}{8}$

    21.

    A

22. Two dozen eggs at 89¢ per dozen are paid for with a $10 bill. The cost is 2×89¢ $= \$1.78$; the change is $\$10 - \$1.78 = \$8.22$.

    A) $1.78   B) $7.22   C) $8.22   D) $9.11

    22.

    C

23. $\frac{1}{7} + \frac{1}{70} + \frac{1}{700} = \frac{100}{700} + \frac{10}{700} + \frac{1}{700} = \frac{111}{700}$.

    A) $\frac{1}{777}$ B) $\frac{3}{777}$ C) $\frac{100}{777}$ D) $\frac{111}{700}$

    23.

    D

24. The angles are in the ratio 1:2:3; $1+2+3 = 6$, so the smallest angle has measure $180° \div 6 = 30°$. The largest angle is $3 \times 30°$.

    A) 30°   B) 60°   C) 90°   D) 120°

    24.

    C

25. 25% of 50% of 100 $= ¼ \times ½ \times 100 = ¼ \times 50 = 12½$.

    A) 12½   B) 25   C) 50   D) 75

    25.

    A

26. A car left from Uphere at 9:00 A.M. and arrived at Downthere, 340 km away, at 1:15 P.M. the same day. The trip took 4¼ hr. The average speed of the car is $340 \div 4¼ = 340 \div 4.25$.

    A) $\frac{340}{7.75}$ B) $\frac{340}{255}$ C) $\frac{340}{415}$ D) $\frac{340}{4.25}$

    26.

    D

27. $\frac{1}{3} + \frac{1}{4} = \frac{7}{12}$. The reciprocal of $\frac{7}{12}$ is $\frac{12}{7}$.

    A) 7   B) $\frac{7}{3}$ C) $\frac{4}{3}$ D) $\frac{12}{7}$

    27.

    D

28. On a certain test, six students scored 75, seven scored 80, eight scored 85, and nine scored 90. The overall average is $(6 \times 75 + 7 \times 80 + 8 \times 85 + 9 \times 90) \div (6+7+8+9) = 2500 \div 30 = 83⅓$.

    A) 80   B) 82½   C) 83⅓   D) 84

    28.

    C

29. Since $\frac{2}{3} \times \frac{3}{2} = 1$ and $\frac{2}{3} \blacksquare \frac{3}{2} = 1$, $\blacksquare$ must really represent $\times$.

    A) $\times$ B) $\div$ C) $+$ D) $-$

    29.

    A

Go on to the next page ⫸ **7**

55

30. Use the converse of the Pythagorean Theorem: $4^2 + 5^2 \neq 6^2$, so B does *not* represent the lengths of the sides of a right triangle. A) 3, 4, 5 B) 4, 5, 6 C) 6, 8, 10 D) 5, 12, 13	30. B
31. $\sqrt{1^3 + 2^3 + 3^3 + 4^3} = \sqrt{1 + 8 + 27 + 64} = \sqrt{100} = 10.$ A) 5 B) 10 C) 100 D) $\sqrt{1000}$	31. B
32. $\frac{6}{5} \times 70 = 6 \times 14 = 84 = 1\frac{1}{3} \times 63.$ A) 60 B) 63 C) 84 D) 112	32. B
33. $\overline{RS} \perp \overline{ST}$ and $m\angle RSQ = 48°$, so $m\angle QST = 90° - 48° = 42°$. Since $\angle PST$ & $\angle QST$ are supplementary, $m\angle PST = 180° - 42°$. A) 132° B) 134° C) 136° D) 138°	33. D
34. The scale of a certain map is ¾ inch = 12 miles. Since 3/4 = 6/8 inch represents 12 miles, ⅝ inch represents 10 miles. The area of this park in square miles is $10^2 = 100$. A) 7.5 B) 10 C) 40 D) 100	34. D
35. The square root of 4/9 is 2/3; the other choices are all smaller. A) $\frac{4}{9}$ B) $\sqrt{\frac{4}{9}}$ C) $(\frac{4}{9})^2$ D) $(\frac{4}{9})^3$	35. B
36. This figure is really a 15×30 rectangle with a 5×20 section removed, so the area is $450 - 100 = 350$. A) 300 B) 325 C) 350 D) 450	36. C
37. 4 hours $= 60 \times 60 \times 4 = 14\,400$ sec; $8/14400 = 1/1800 = (1/18)\%$. A) 2% B) $\frac{1}{2}\%$ C) $\frac{1}{9}\%$ D) $\frac{1}{18}\%$	37. D
38. The sum of the squares of three whole numbers is 165. Since $165 = 10^2 + 8^2 + 1^2$ or $10^2 + 7^2 + 4^2$, the largest is $10^2 = 100$. A) 100 B) 121 C) 144 D) 160	38. A
39. Each types 150 letters in 3 days or 50 per day. Therefore, two (together) can type 100 letters in 1 day. A) 90 B) 100 C) 120 D) 150	39. B
40. $1 + 2 + 3 + \ldots + 99 + 100 = 5050$; $(1 + 3 + 5 + \ldots + 197 + 199) = 2 \times (1 + 2 + 3 + \ldots + 99 + 100) - (1 + 1 + 1 + \ldots + 1 + 1) = 10100 - 100.$ A) 10 000 B) 10 050 C) 10 100 D) 10 150	40. A

The end of the contest ✍ **7**

Solutions

1981-82 Annual 7th Grade Contest

Tuesday, February 9, 1982

7

Contest Information

- **Solutions** Turn the page for detailed contest solutions (written in the question boxes) and letter answers (written in the *Answers* column to the right of each question).

- **Scores** Please remember that *this is a contest, not a test*—and there is no "passing" or "failing" score. Few students score as high as 30 points (75% correct). Students with half that, 15 points, *should be commended!*

- **Answers & Rating Scale** Turn to page 86 for the letter answers to each question and the rating scale for this contest.

		Answers
1.	$111+222+333+444 = 111\times(1+2+3+4) = 111\times10 = 1110$. A) 1000 B) 1010 C) 1110 D) 101010	1. C
2.	$\frac{1}{4} = \frac{25}{100} = 0.25$, so choice B is correct. A) 0.2 B) 0.25 C) 0.4 D) 0.5	2. B
3.	The smallest sum is $100000 + 100000 = 200000$ and the largest sum is $999999 + 999999 = 1999999$; so choice B is correct. A) 5 digits B) 7 digits C) 8 digits D) 12 digits	3. B
4.	$10^3 + 10^2 + 10^1 + 1 = 1000 + 100 + 10 + 1 = 1111$. A) 10^6 B) 40^6 C) 1110 D) 1111	4. D
5.	In a right triangle, the measure of one angle is $55°$. The measure of the smallest angle of this triangle is $90° - 55° = 35°$. A) $1°$ B) $25°$ C) $35°$ D) $90°$	5. C
6.	$\frac{1111}{11} = 1111\div11 = (1100+11)\div11 = 100+1 = 101$. A) 11 B) 100 C) 101 D) 111	6. C
7.	$19.82 - 18.92 = (18.82 + 1.0) - (18.82 + 0.1) = 1.0 - 0.1 = 0.9$. A) 0.1 B) 0.9 C) 1.1 D) 1.9	7. B
8.	3% of $900 = 3/100\times900 = 3\times9 = 27$. A) 30 B) 27 C) 9 D) 3	8. B
9.	$\sqrt{25} - \sqrt{16} = 5 - 4 = 1$, so choice A is correct. A) 1 B) 3 C) 9 D) 11	9. A
10.	Since $m\angle AOC + m\angle BOC = 180°$ and $m\angle BOC = 48°$, $m\angle AOC = 180° - 48° = 132°$. A) $48°$ B) $132°$ C) $142°$ D) $312°$	10. B
11.	Since 2 pounds = 32 ounces and the pizza is cut into 8 congruent pieces, the weight of three slices is $(32\div8)\times3 = 12$ ounces. A) 3 ounces B) 6 ounces C) 8 ounces D) 12 ounces	11. D
12.	$6\frac{1}{4} - 5\frac{3}{4} = (6\frac{1}{4} - 5) - (5\frac{3}{4} - 1) = 1\frac{1}{4} - \frac{3}{4}$. A) $\frac{1}{4} - 5\frac{3}{4}$ B) $1\frac{3}{4} - \frac{1}{4}$ C) $1\frac{1}{4} - \frac{3}{4}$ D) $6 - 5$	12. C
13.	3600 seconds = $(3600\div60)$ minutes = 60 minutes = 1 hour. 1 hour from 1 P.M. is 2 P.M. A) 1 A.M. B) 2 P.M. C) 3 P.M. D) 4 P.M.	13. B
14.	$2 + 2 \times 2 - 2 = 2 + (2 \times 2) - 2 = 2 + 4 - 2 = 4$. A) 0 B) 2 C) 4 D) 6	14. C
15.	The area of the square is $8^2 = 64$. The area of the shaded region is $\frac{1}{4}\times64 = 16$. A) 4 B) 8 C) 16 D) 64	15. C

Go on to the next page ⟩ **7**

16. $\frac{1}{2} + \frac{2}{3} + \frac{3}{4} = \frac{6}{12} + \frac{8}{12} + \frac{9}{12} = \frac{23}{12}$. A) $\frac{23}{12}$ B) $\frac{6}{9}$ C) $\frac{6}{24}$ D) $\frac{47}{24}$	16. A
17. $5.1 \div 0.017 = 5100 \div 17 = 300$, so choice B is correct. A) 30 B) 300 C) 3000 D) 30000	17. B
18. $(56 \times 71) + (56 \times 29) = 56 \times (71 + 29) = 56 \times (100) = = 5600$. A) 5500 B) 5580 C) 5590 D) 5600	18. D
19. $28{:}70 = (28 \div 7){:}(70 \div 7) = 4{:}10 = (11 \times 4){:}(11 \times 10) = 44{:}110$; in 110 times at bats, Alice should have 44 hits. A) 44 B) 48 C) 68 D) 72	19. A
20. $\frac{1}{2} \div \frac{1}{4} = \frac{1}{2} \times 4 = 2$. A) $\frac{1}{8}$ B) $\frac{1}{4}$ C) $\frac{1}{2}$ D) 2	20. D
21. Two sides of a triangle have lengths of 16 and 18. Sum of the lengths of *any* 2 sides is greater than the 3rd side, so 3rd $\neq$ 1. A) 30 B) 17 C) 7 D) 1	21. D
22. $2^5 + 4^3 + 5^2 = = 32 + 64 + 25 = 121 = 11^2$. A) 11^{11} B) 11^{10} C) 11^5 D) 11^2	22. D
23. A worker's daily salary is increased from \$40 to \$50. This is an increase of \$10; since $10/40 = 1/4$, the percent increase is 25%. A) 50% B) 25% C) 20% D) 10%	23. B
24. $\left(\frac{1}{3} - \frac{1}{4}\right) - \left(\frac{1}{6} - \frac{1}{12}\right) = \left(\frac{4}{12} - \frac{3}{12}\right) - \left(\frac{2}{12} - \frac{1}{12}\right) = \frac{1}{12} - \frac{1}{12} = 0$. A) 0 B) $\frac{1}{24}$ C) $\frac{1}{12}$ D) $\frac{1}{6}$	24. A
25. Use units' digit: $7 \times 4 \times 1 = 28$, so units' digit is 8. A) 207204858 B) 207204859 C) 207204861 D) 207204862	25. A
26. Sue's present age + 30 years = $1\frac{1}{2}$ times her present age, so $\frac{1}{2}$ her present age is 30 and Sue is now $2 \times 30 = 60$ years old. A) 15 B) 20 C) 45 D) 60	26. D
27. Since 5 cm represents 40 meters, 1 cm represents $40 \div 5 = 8$ meters and $6\frac{3}{4}$ cm represents $6\frac{3}{4} \times 8 = 54$ meters. A) 51 meters B) 54 meters C) 57 meters D) 60 meters	27. B
28. If 10 men can build a house in 60 days, then 20 men can build the same house in half the time or 30 days. A) 30 days B) 60 days C) 90 days D) 120 days	28. A
29. The cost of a tire and a jack is \$110. If the tire cost \$100 more than the jack, the jack cost \$5 and the tire cost \$105. A) \$5 B) \$10 C) \$100 D) \$105	29. D

Go on to the next page ⫸ **7**

30.	For a car to make a 20 mile trip at an average rate of 30 miles per hour, it must complete the trip in $20 \div 30 = \frac{2}{3}$ of an hour. A) 20 minutes B) 30 minutes C) 40 minutes D) 50 minutes	30. C
31.	The measure of the largest angle in a triangle can *never* be $< 60°$. A) 59° B) 61° C) 178° D) 179°30′	31. A
32.	50% of 50% of $50 = 0.5 \times 0.5 \times 50 = 0.25 \times 50 = 25\%$ of 50. A) 100% B) 50% C) 25% D) 12.5%	32. C
33.	A store buys pens at 8 for 25¢ and sells them at 2 for 15¢ or 8 for 60¢. Profit on 8 pens is 35¢; so profit on 80 pens is $3.50. A) 10 pens B) 40 pens C) 80 pens D) 100 pens	33. C
34.	$\dfrac{2^{150}}{2^{50}} = 2^{150-50} = 2^{100}$, so choice D is correct. A) 3 B) 100 C) 2^3 D) 2^{100}	34. D
35.	$1 + 2 + 3 + 4 + 6 + 8 + 12 + 24 = 60$. A) 24 B) 48 C) 36 D) 60	35. D
36.	The second hand goes once around the clock each *minute*, not each second. In 60 minutes, it goes $60 \times 10\pi = 600\pi$ cm. A) $36\,000\pi$ cm B) $6\,000\pi$ cm C) $3\,600\pi$ cm D) 600π cm	36. D
37.	$\boxed{3} + \triangle_2 - \boxed{\triangle_4} = \boxed{7} + 6 - \,_{16}\! = 49 + 6 - 20 = 35.$ A) 75 B) 35 C) 32 D) 9	37. B
38.	The diagram shows how to divide the garden. The inner square is 2 m ×2 m; each surrounding rectangle is 4 m ×6 m. A) 3 m×3 m B) 8 m×3 m C) 4 m×6 m D) 2 m×12 m	38. C
39.	One skip = 4 hops, and 1 jump = 2 skips = 8 hops. A hop, skip, and a jump $= 1 + 4 + 8 = 13$ hops. A) 7 B) 8 C) 12 D) 13	39. D
40.	The owl went up 18 units each day and down 13 units each night. By night 14, the owl's net movement was 70 units. On day 15, the owl climbed to 88 units; at night it fell back to 75. It got to 93 units on day 16, its *first* time at the top. A) day 16 B) day 17 C) day 18 D) day 19	40. A

The end of the contest ✍ **7**

Solutions

1977-78 Annual 8th Grade Contest

Tuesday, February 14, 1978

8

Contest Information

- **Solutions** Turn the page for detailed contest solutions (written in the question boxes) and letter answers (written in the *Answers* column to the right of each question).

- **Scores** Please remember that *this is a contest, not a test*—and there is no "passing" or "failing" score. Few students score as high as 30 points (75% correct). Students with half that, 15 points, *should be commended!*

- **Answers & Rating Scale** Turn to page 87 for the letter answers to each question and the rating scale for this contest.

1. 32% is the same as 0.32 = 32/100 = (32÷4)/(100÷4) = 8/25. A) 32 B) $3\frac{1}{8}$ C) $\frac{8}{25}$ D) none of these	1. C
2. 217 is *not* divisible by 3, 9, or 11. A) 3 B) 9 C) 11 D) none of these	2. D
3. The set of common elements is {1, 3}, so choice D is correct. A) {1, 2, 3, 5, 7} B) {1} C) ∅ D) none of these	3. D
4. An isosceles right triangle has 1 angle of 90° and 2 angles of 45°. A) 45° B) 60° C) 180° D) none of these	4. A
5. $2^4 \times 5^4 = (2 \times 5)^4 = 10^4 = 10\,000$. A) 320 B) 2 000 C) 10 000 D) none of these	5. C
6. 55/44 = 5/4 = (5×25)/(4×25) = 125/100 = 125%. A) 125% B) 120% C) 80% D) 75%	6. A
7. The sum of 2 numbers is 10. Their product is at most 5×5 = 25. A) 9 B) 10 C) 25 D) none of these	7. C
8. The perimeter is 32, so each side is 8 and the area is 8×8 = 64. A) 16 B) 32 C) 64 D) none of these	8. C
9. 7.63 + 9.32 = 16.95; round up to 17.0. A) 16.9 B) 17.0 C) 17.9 D) none of these	9. B
10. 11, 31, & 41 are primes; 1 is *not* a prime, 21 = 3×7, & 51 = 3×17. A) 3 B) 4 C) 5 D) none of these	10. A
11. A circle's area is $\pi r^2 = \pi(d/2)^2 = \pi d^2/4$. A) $\frac{\pi d^2}{4}$ B) $\frac{\pi d^2}{2}$ C) πd^2 D) $2\pi d$	11. A
12. 91 = 7×13 and 93 = 3×31, but 97 is prime. A) 91 B) 93 C) 97 D) none of these	12. C
13. Every integer is a real number. A) irrational B) real C) positive D) non-negative	13. B
14. $(6 \times 10^4) + (5 \times 10^2) + (3 \times 10^1) = 60\,000 + 500 + 30 = 60\,530$. A) 653 B) 6053 C) 356 D) none of these	14. D
15. The inequality $3x - 1 < 11$ is satisfied by only 2 & 3. Choice A is incomplete, choice B includes 4, & choice C is incorrect. A) 2 B) 2, 3, and 4 C) 5 D) none of these	15. D

Go on to the next page ⫸ **8**

16. $4\frac{1}{6} \div 1\frac{2}{3} = \frac{25}{6} \div \frac{5}{3} = \frac{25}{6} \times \frac{3}{5} = \frac{5}{2} = 2\frac{1}{2}$.

    A) $2\frac{1}{2}$ B) $\frac{2}{5}$ C) $2\frac{1}{5}$ D) none of these

16. A

17. 5 is the only solution to I but every integer satisfies II.

     I. $x + 15 = 20$ II. $5x \neq 14$

     A) I, not II   B) II, not I   C) I and II   D) none of these

17. A

18. $8 \div 2 \times 4 = 4 \times 4 = 16$.

     A) 64   B) 16   C) 4   D) 1

18. B

19. $1+4 = 5 \neq$ perf. sq.; $\sqrt{4} = 2 \neq$ perf. sq.; $4 \times 9 = 36 =$ perf. sq.

     A) addition   B) multiplication

     C) square-rooting   D) none of these

19. B

20. From right to left, place values are 1, 6^1, 6^2, and 6^3; $2 \times 36 = 72$.

     A) 36   B) 72   C) 200   D) 216

20. B

21. At most $a = 9$, $b = 4$, & $a + b < 20$; use $a = 1$ & $b = 4$ for others.

     A) $a > b$ B) $a - b = 5$ C) $a = 2b$ D) $a + b < 20$

21. D

22. $511 = 7 \times 73$, so $3 \leq p \leq 9$.

     A) $18 \leq p \leq 23$ B) $10 \leq p \leq 17$ C) $3 \leq p \leq 9$ D) none of these

22. C

23. $9.6{:}8 = 96{:}80 = 48{:}40 = 24{:}20 = 12{:}10 = 6{:}5$.

     A) 6:5   B) 12:1   C) 1:12   D) none of these

23. A

24. $5\S(3\S4) = 5\S\frac{3+4}{3 \times 4} = 5\S\frac{7}{12} = \frac{5 + 7/12}{5 \times 7/12} = \frac{67/12}{35/12} = \frac{67}{35} = 1\frac{32}{35}$.

     A) $1\frac{22}{35}$ B) $2\frac{11}{12}$ C) $5\frac{7}{12}$ D) none of these

24. D

25. $a/b > c/d$ if $a \times d > b \times c$; choices A, B, & C are all true.

     A) $\frac{2}{9} > \frac{1}{5}$ B) $\frac{5}{7} < \frac{8}{9}$ C) $\frac{2}{7} > \frac{1}{4}$ D) none of these

25. D

26. $87\frac{1}{2}\% = 7/8$; 56 is 7/8 of 64.

     A) 35   B) 49   C) 64   D) none of these

26. C

27. If the lengths of the legs are 10 and 24, the length of the hypotenuse is the square root of $10^2 + 24^2 = 26$.

     A) 17   B) 26   C) 34   D) 38

27. B

28. If $N = 6$, $N/2 + 1 = 4$ & $N/2 + 3 = 6$. If $N = 4$, $N/2 + 2 = 4$.

     A) $\frac{N}{2} + 1$ B) $\frac{N}{2} + 2$ C) $\frac{N}{2} + 3$ D) none of these

28. D

29. If the union is B, A must have only elements that are also in B.

     A) A is a subset of B B) $A = \varnothing$

     C) $A = B$ D) none of these

29. A

Go on to the next page ⟫ **8**

30. Try a few pairs of numbers like 76 and 67. The difference is *always* divisible by 9. A) 2 B) 4 C) 6 D) none of these	30. D
31. If $\frac{1}{3}$ is N, then $\frac{1}{6} = \frac{1}{2} \times \frac{1}{3}$ is $\frac{1}{2}N$ & $\frac{5}{6}$ is $5 \times \frac{1}{2}N = 2.5N$. A) 1.2N B) 2.5N C) 3N D) none of these	31. B
32. When expressed as a percent, $0.03\frac{1}{3} = (0.03\frac{1}{3} \times 100)\% = 3\frac{1}{3}\%$. A) $33\frac{1}{3}\%$ B) $3\frac{1}{3}\%$ C) $0.03\frac{1}{3}\%$ D) none of these	32. B
33. Square a number with 2 decimal places. The result has 4 decimal places. Reverse the process for this problem. A) 2 B) 3 C) 4 D) 5	33. A
34. If a girl with an allowance of \$X spends \$Y, she has \$(X - Y) left and the fractional part that she did *not* spend is $(X - Y)/X$. A) $\frac{X-Y}{X}$ B) $X - Y$ C) $\frac{Y}{X}$ D) none of these	34. A
35. The man began with \$162, spent \$108, then lost two-thirds of of the remaining \$54, which left him with \$18. A) \$42 B) \$50 C) \$81 D) none of these	35. D
36. Solve the proportion $88/60 = 1100/?$. This is equivalent to $60 \times 1100 = 88 \times ?$. Since $6600 = 88 \times 750$, choice A is correct. A) 750 mph B) 740 mph C) 730 mph D) none of these	36. A
37. $a/b < c/d$ if $a \times d < b \times c$; thus, choice B is correct. A) $\frac{11}{15}, \frac{13}{19}, \frac{13}{23}$ B) $\frac{13}{23}, \frac{13}{19}, \frac{11}{15}$ C) $\frac{13}{23}, \frac{11}{15}, \frac{13}{19}$ D) none of these	37. B
38. The fraction with the largest numerator and smallest denominator is choice B. This must be the largest fraction listed. A) $\frac{n}{m}$ B) $\frac{n+1}{m-1}$ C) $\frac{n-1}{m}$ D) $\frac{n}{m+1}$	38. B
39. If $3N = 5$, then $3N \div 5 = 5 \div 5$ or $3N/5 = 1$. A) $\frac{5}{3}$ B) $\frac{3N}{5}$ C) 0.6 D) none of these	39. B
40. 4 pens:C¢ = 4÷C pens:1¢ = 40×4/C pens:40¢ = 160/C pens:40¢. A) 10C B) $\frac{10}{C}$ C) $\frac{160}{C}$ D) none of these	40. C

The end of the contest ✍ **8**

Solutions

1978-79 Annual 8th Grade Contest

Tuesday, February 13, 1979

8

Contest Information

- **Solutions** Turn the page for detailed contest solutions (written in the question boxes) and letter answers (written in the *Answers* column to the right of each question).

- **Scores** Please remember that *this is a contest, not a test*—and there is no "passing" or "failing" score. Few students score as high as 30 points (75% correct). Students with half that, 15 points, *should be commended!*

- **Answers & Rating Scale** Turn to page 88 for the letter answers to each question and the rating scale for this contest.

1. $1.23 + 0.046 = 1.230 + 0.046 = 1.276.$
    A) 1.2346   B) 1.276   C) 1.69   D) 5.83

2. 365 days = 52 weeks 1 day; 1 day before Tuesday is Monday.
    A) Sunday   B) Monday   C) Tuesday   D) Wednesday

3. $\frac{11}{12} - \frac{2}{3} = \frac{11}{12} - \frac{8}{12} = \frac{3}{12} = \frac{1}{4}.$

    A) $\frac{1}{4}$ B) $\frac{9}{12}$ C) 1   D) $\frac{9}{4}$

4. In a right triangle, if one acute angle has a measure of 35°, the other acute angle has a measure of $90° - 35° = 55°$.
    A) 55°   B) 65°   C) 90°   D) 145°

5. $(-8) - (-13) = (-8) + 13 = 13 - 8 = 5.$
    A) −21   B) −5   C) 5   D) 21

6. The sum of the digits of $7\,000\,000\,000\,002$ is 9, so remainder is 0.
    A) 0   B) 1   C) 2   D) 8

7. $(2.1)^2 - (0.1)^2 = (2.1 \times 2.1) - (0.1 \times 0.1) = 4.41 - 0.01 = 4.40 = 4.4.$
    A) 4.4   B) 4.1   C) 4.0   D) 3.9

8. 50% of $\frac{3}{7} = \frac{1}{2} \times \frac{3}{7} = \frac{3}{14}; \frac{3}{7} + \frac{3}{14} = \frac{6}{14} + \frac{3}{14} = \frac{9}{14}.$

    A) $\frac{4}{7}$ B) $\frac{5}{7}$ C) $\frac{7}{10}$ D) $\frac{9}{14}$

9. $\frac{8}{9} \div \frac{4}{3} = \frac{8}{9} \times \frac{3}{4} = \frac{24}{36} = \frac{2}{3}.$

    A) $\frac{32}{27}$ B) $\frac{2}{3}$ C) $\frac{2}{27}$ D) 6

10. If $280 = N$, then $350 = 5/4 \times 280 = 5/4 \times N = 5N/4.$

    A) $\frac{N}{4}$ B) $\frac{4N}{5}$ C) $\frac{4N}{3}$ D) $\frac{5N}{4}$

11. Pair 1 & 1000, 2 & 999, 3 & 998, . . . , 499 & 502, and 500 & 501. Each pair has an average of 500.5, so choice C is correct.
    A) 499.5   B) 500.0   C) 500.5   D) 501.0

12. 15 cm:3 m = 15 cm:300 cm = $(15 \div 5):(300 \div 5) = 3:60 = 1:20.$
    A) 1:20   B) 1:5   C) 5:1   D) 20:1

13. If $a = 3$ and $b = -4$, then $\frac{2a - b}{a + b} = \frac{(2 \times 3) - (-4)}{3 + (-4)} = \frac{6 + 4}{-1} = -10.$

    A) −10   B) −2   C) 2   D) $1\frac{3}{7}$

14. If the area of a square is 100, each side is 10 and perimeter is 40.
    A) 10   B) 25   C) 40   D) 400

15. $10 + 20 \div 2 + 3 = 10 + (20 \div 2) + 3 = 10 + 10 + 3 = 23.$
    A) 6   B) 14   C) 18   D) 23

Go on to the next page ⫸ **8**

16. $N = 6+4+3+1+\frac{1}{3}N$, so $N = 14+\frac{1}{3}N$; thus, $\frac{2}{3}N = 14$ & $N = 21$. | 16.

    A) 12   B) 15   C) 18   D) 21   D

17. A tennis player uses up 800 calories every hour. In 1 hour and 15 minutes, this player uses $1\frac{1}{4} \times 800 = 1000$ calories. | 17. B

    A) 900   B) 1000   C) 1100   D) 1200

18. If $3a = 5b$, then a could equal 5 & b could equal 3; so $a{:}b = 5{:}3$. | 18. C

    A) 3:5   B) 3:8   C) 5:3   D) 8:3

19. Add the 1st 8 positive odds:$1+3+5+7+9+11+13+15 = 64$. | 19. C

    A) 4   B) 6   C) 8   D) 16

20. $10 \times 15 \times 24 = 3600 = 60 \times 60$, so choice A is correct. | 20. A

    A) 60   B) 80   C) 800   D) 6000

21. If $3x - 6y = 8$, then $3(x - 2y) = 8$ and $x - 2y = 8 \div 3 = 8/3$. | 21. C

    A) 4   B) 3   C) $2\frac{2}{3}$ D) 5

22. The product of an odd number of -1's is -1. | 22. A

    A) -1 B) 1   C) 1979   D) -1979

23. Suppose both dimensions were 10 originally. The new dimensions are 12 and 9; the new area is 108, an increase of 8%. | 23. B

    A) 2%   B) 8%   C) 10%   D) 20%

24. $\dfrac{\frac{1}{2}+\frac{1}{3}}{\frac{1}{2}-\frac{1}{3}} = \dfrac{\frac{3}{6}+\frac{2}{6}}{\frac{3}{6}-\frac{2}{6}} = \frac{5}{6} \div \frac{1}{6} = \frac{5}{6} \times \frac{6}{1} = 5$. | 24. D

    A) $\frac{1}{6}$ B) 1   C) $\frac{5}{6}$ D) 5

25. If N is an even integer, then $3N$ is even and $3N + 3$ is odd. | 25. D

    A) $\frac{1}{2}N$ B) $\frac{1}{2}N + 1$ C) $3N$ D) $3N + 3$

26. $0.\overline{666} = 2/3$ and $0.\overline{333} = 1/3$; their sum is $3/3 = 1$. | 26. D

    A) 0.9   B) 99%   C) $\frac{9999}{10000}$ D) 1

27. $100 \times 100 = 10000$ and $1000 \times 1000 = 1000000$; the product must have at least 5 digits and must have fewer than 7 digits. | 27. C

    A) 3 digits   B) 4 digits   C) 6 digits   D) 9 digits

28. Since $\frac{1}{9} \times \frac{1}{9} = \frac{1}{81}$, $\frac{1}{9}$ is the square root of $\frac{1}{81}$. | 28. D

    A) $\frac{1}{3}$ B) $\frac{2}{9}$ C) $\frac{1}{18}$ D) $\frac{1}{81}$

29. Since $4 \times 5 \times 10 = 200 = 2 \times 100$, the final 2 digits of the product $4 \times 5 \times 6 \times 7 \times 8 \times 9 \times 10 \times 11 \times 12 \times 13 \times 14$ are 00. | 29. A

    A) 0   B) 2   C) 4   D) 8

Go on to the next page ▐▐▐▶ **8**

30. A girl walks $\frac{3}{4}$ of the way home in 18 minutes. Since $\frac{1}{4} = \frac{1}{3} \times \frac{3}{4}$, she can walk the rest of the way home, $\frac{1}{4}$, in $\frac{1}{3} \times 18 = 6$ mins.

    A) $4\frac{1}{2}$ minutes B) 6 minutes   C) 9 minutes   D) 24 minutes

    30.
    B

31. If the radius is 2, the area is 4π. If the radius is doubled, the area is 16π. The area has increased by $16\pi - 4\pi = 12\pi$.

    A) 16π B) 12π C) 8π D) 4π

    31.
    B

32. $\S(3 + \uparrow 2\uparrow)\S = \S(3 + 2^2 + 1)\S = \S 8 \S = \frac{1}{8}$.

    A) $\frac{1}{8}$ B) $\frac{8}{15}$ C) $\frac{7}{12}$ D) $\frac{16}{3}$

    32.
    A

33. Try $a = 2$ & 3 and $b = -3$ & -2. Only choice C is always true.

    A) $-a < b$ B) $a < -b$ C) $b - a < 0$ D) $ab > 0$

    33.
    C

34. Since 10 boys can play for 36 minutes, 360 minutes of play time is available. If 24 boys share this time equally, each boy gets (360 minutes)$\div 24 = 15$ minutes.

    A) 12   B) 15   C) 18   D) 20

    34.
    B

35. Since $6^2 + 8^2 = 10^2$, the triangle is a right triangle. Using one leg as the base and the other as the height, area $= \frac{1}{2} \times 6 \times 8 = 24$.

    A) 24   B) 30   C) 40   D) 48

    35.
    A

36. If $\begin{vmatrix} a & b \\ c & d \end{vmatrix}$ means $ad - bc$, $\begin{vmatrix} 5 & 4 \\ 2 & 3 \end{vmatrix} = (5 \times 3) - (4 \times 2) = 15 - 8 = 7$.

    A) 2   B) 7   C) 14   D) 22

    36.
    B

37. 15 people with brown hair have non-brown eyes, 6 with brown eyes have non-brown hair, and 23 with brown hair have brown eyes. This accounts for 44 people, leaving 6 with neither trait.

    A) 6   B) 8   C) 10   D) 12

    37.
    A

38. Split the figure as shown. Each triangle has an area is 6 and the rectangle has an area of 32. Total area is 12 + 32 = 44.

    A) 44   B) 48   C) 90   D) 100

    38.
    A

39. Every team plays 18 games. Each game is played by 2 teams. The number of games is $\frac{1}{2}(18 \times 10) = 90$.

    A) 20   B) 45   C) 90   D) 180

    39.
    C

40. $a \times b \times a = a^2 \times b = a^3 \times \frac{b}{a} = a^3 \div \frac{a}{b} = a^3 \P \frac{a}{b}$, so $\P$ is really division.

    A) $\div$ B) $\times$ C) $+$ D) $-$

    40.
    A

The end of the contest ✍️ **8**

Solutions

1979-80 Annual 8th Grade Contest

Tuesday, February 12, 1980

8

Contest Information

- **Solutions** Turn the page for detailed contest solutions (written in the question boxes) and letter answers (written in the *Answers* column to the right of each question).

- **Scores** Please remember that *this is a contest, not a test*—and there is no "passing" or "failing" score. Few students score as high as 30 points (75% correct). Students with half that, 15 points, *should be commended!*

- **Answers & Rating Scale** Turn to page 89 for the letter answers to each question and the rating scale for this contest.

1. $5\frac{1}{2} - 2\frac{3}{4} = 5\frac{2}{4} - 2\frac{3}{4} = 4\frac{6}{4} - 2\frac{3}{4} = 2\frac{3}{4}$ A) $2\frac{3}{4}$ B) $3\frac{1}{4}$ C) $3\frac{1}{2}$ D) $3\frac{3}{4}$	1. A
2. Rewrite choices C and D as 6.010 and 6.100; choice B is nearest.. A) 5.985 B) 6.005 C) 6.01 D) 6.1	2. B
3. The reciprocal of the reciprocal of the number is the original #. A) $1\frac{1}{2}$ B) $\frac{3}{4}$ C) $\frac{2}{3}$ D) $\frac{1}{2}$	3. A
4. The rectangular solid has dimensions $3 \times 4 \times 5$; therefore, 60 small cubical cubical blocks would fill it. A) 47 B) 48 C) 60 D) 94	4. C
5. There are 30 days in June; 10% of 30 = 1/10×30 = 3. A) 10 days B) 6 days C) 3 days D) no days	5. C
6. 0.40 = 40/100 = 4/10 = 2/5. A) $\frac{1}{25}$ B) $\frac{1}{4}$ C) $\frac{1}{40}$ D) $\frac{2}{5}$	6. D
7. There are 99 such numbers from 1 to 99; from 10 to 99 is 9 fewer. A) 90 B) 91 C) 99 D) 89	7. A
8. $\frac{6}{7} = \frac{6 \times 2}{7 \times 2}$, since numerator and denominator are *multiplied* by 2. A) $\frac{6-2}{7-2}$ B) $\frac{6 \times 6}{7 \times 7}$ C) $\frac{6+2}{7+2}$ D) $\frac{6 \times 2}{7 \times 2}$	8. D
9. $(-\frac{1}{2}) \times (-\frac{2}{3}) \times (-\frac{3}{4}) \times (-\frac{4}{5}) = \frac{1}{2} \times \frac{2}{3} \times \frac{3}{4} \times \frac{4}{5} = \frac{1}{5}$. A) $\frac{1}{5}$ B) $\frac{1}{2}$ C) $-\frac{1}{2}$ D) $-\frac{1}{5}$	9. A
10. July 4 is (25+30+4) days = 59 days = 8 weeks 3 days later. A) Sunday B) Monday C) Thursday D) Friday	10. D
11. The top number is the sum of 347 and 563. ?1? Since their sum is 910, the missing digits are −347 are 9 and 0 and their sum is 9 + 0 = 9. 563 A) 7 B) 8 C) 9 D) 10	11. C
12. $2 + (6 \times 6) - (3 \times 2) + 1 = 2 + 36 - 6 + 1 = 33$. A) 29 B) 33 C) 39 D) 91	12. B
13. A string in the shape of a 2×8 rectangle has a length of 20. This is the perimeter of the square, so its side is 5. A) 5 B) 4 C) 16 D) 20	13. A
14. $52/39 = (52 \div 13)/(39 \div 13) = 4/3 = (4/3) \times 100\% = 133\frac{1}{3}\%$. A) $66\frac{2}{3}$ B) 75% C) 120% D) $133\frac{1}{3}\%$	14. D

Go on to the next page ⫸ **8**

15. $(2^2)^2 = 4^2 = 16$, so choice C is correct. A) 6 B) 8 C) 16 D) 64	15. C
16. The sum of the two smaller sides must be greater than the 3rd. A) 7 cm B) 8 cm C) 25 cm D) 26 cm	16. B
17. $5 \times 6 \times 7 = 210$; $5^2 + 6^2 + 7^2 = 25+36+49 = 110$; others are less. A) $5 + 6 + 7$ B) $5 \times 6 \times 7$ C) $\sqrt{5} + \sqrt{6} + \sqrt{7}$ D) $5^2 + 6^2 + 7^2$	17. B
18. If $x + 2 = y$ and $y + 1 = 5$, then $y = 4$ and $x + 2 = 4$; $x = 2$. A) 1 B) 2 C) 3 D) 4	18. B
19. The sum of the digits of 5470126♦3 is divisible by 9 if ♦ = 8. A) 0 B) 3 C) 6 D) 8	19. D
20. $1.6 + 0.16 + 0.016 = 1.600 + 0.160 + 0.016 = 1.776$. A) 1.616 B) 1.666 C) 1.676 D) 1.776	20. D
21. The least common multiple of 3, 4, and 6 is 12. Thus, once in every 12 days, all three will call on the same day. A) 9 B) 12 C) 13 D) 15	21. B
22. $(-1)+(-1) \times (-1) \div (-1) = (-1)+1 \div (-1) = (-1)+(-1) = -2$. A) -2 B) -1 C) 0 D) 1	22. A
23. If $e = mc^2$, then $(e)^2 = (mc^2)^2$ or $e^2 = m^2c^4$. Thus, $\dfrac{e^2}{m^2c^4} = 1$. A) e^2 B) 2 C) 1 D) ½	23. C
24. $22.5{:}225 = (22.5 \div 10){:}(225 \div 10) = 2.25{:}22.5$, so choice C is correct. A) 0.0225 B) 0.225 C) 2.25 D) 225	24. C
25. Since the area of the 5 squares is 180, each has an area of $180 \div 5 = 36$. A side of each square is 6 and the perimeter of the figure is $12 \times 6 = 72$. A) 36 B) 45 C) 72 D) 120	25. C
26. 21, 39, and 51 are *all* divisible by 3. Only choice D has a pair of prime numbers which differ by 2. A) 19 and 21 B) 39 and 41 C) 49 and 51 D) 59 and 61	26. D
27. $\dfrac{1}{0.1} + \dfrac{2}{0.2} + \dfrac{3}{0.3} + \dfrac{4}{0.4} = \dfrac{10}{1} + \dfrac{20}{2} + \dfrac{30}{3} + \dfrac{40}{4} = 10+10+10+10$. A) 40 B) 10 C) 0.4 D) 0.1	27. A
28. The sum of the first n odd numbers is n^2. The sum of the first 30 odd numbers is $30^2 = 900$. A) 60 B) 90 C) 300 D) 900	28. D
29. The sum of the adults' scores is $20 \times 80 = 1600$; the sum of the teenagers' scores is $30 \times 70 = 2100$. Average is $(3700) \div 50 = 74\%$. A) 73% B) 74% C) 75% D) 76%	29. B

Go on to the next page ⃗ **8**

30. $\dfrac{1}{2+\dfrac{3}{4+\dfrac{5}{6}}} = \dfrac{1}{2+\dfrac{3}{\dfrac{29}{6}}} = \dfrac{1}{2+\dfrac{18}{29}} = \dfrac{1}{\dfrac{76}{29}} = \dfrac{29}{76}.$

   A) $\dfrac{29}{76}$ B) $\dfrac{76}{29}$ C) $\dfrac{20}{29}$ D) $\dfrac{29}{20}$

30.

A

31. $x+y = \dfrac{7}{10}$ & $x-y = \dfrac{5}{14}$; so $x^2-y^2 = (x+y)(x-y) = \dfrac{7}{10} \times \dfrac{5}{14} = \dfrac{1}{4}.$

   A) $(\tfrac{7}{10})^2-(\tfrac{5}{14})^2$ B) $(\tfrac{1}{2})^2$ C) $(\tfrac{5}{14})^2$ D) $(\tfrac{7}{10} - \tfrac{5}{14})^2$

31.

B

32. $\dfrac{1}{4} = \dfrac{4}{16}$ and $\dfrac{1}{3} = \dfrac{4}{12}$; $\dfrac{4}{13}$ is between them.

   A) $\dfrac{1}{7}$ B) $\dfrac{4}{13}$ C) $\dfrac{6}{17}$ D) $\dfrac{6}{25}$

32.

B

33. The perimeter of the window consists of 3 sides of the rectangle plus the circumference of a semi-circle of radius 3. Perimeter $= 8 + 8 + 6 + 3\pi$ $= 22 + 3\pi$.

   A) $22 + 18\pi$ B) $22 + 9\pi$ C) $22 + 6\pi$ D) $22 + 3\pi$

33.

D

34. On each \$100, the shopkeeper makes \$20. Thus, the profit is \$20 for a cost of \$80. Since $20/80 = 1/4 = 25\%$, choice B is correct.

   A) 20%   B) 25%   C) 40%   D) 80%

34.

B

35. $[(-5) \ast 2] \ast 4 = [-5+2+\tfrac{-10}{10}] \ast 4 = [-4] \ast 4 = -4+4+\tfrac{-16}{10} = -1.6.$

   A) 15.2   B) –13.8   C) –1.6   D) 0

35.

C

36. Twelve 5-liter cans, filled with syrup, weigh 492 units. Each can, filled with syrup, weighs $492 \div 12 = 41$ units. The weight of 1 liter of syrup (*without* a can of 3 units) is $(41 - 3) \div 5 = 7.6$ units.

   A) 5 units   B) 6.5 units   C) 7.5 units   D) 8 units

36.

C

37. $\dfrac{20}{30} = \dfrac{2}{3} = \sqrt{\dfrac{4}{9}} = \sqrt{\dfrac{20}{45}}$, so choice C is correct.

   A) 9   B) 30   C) 45   D) 900

37.

C

38. If radius is 10, area is 100π. If radius is decreased 10% to 9, area is 81π. This is a decrease of 19π from 100π or 19%.

   A) 19%   B) 20%   C) 21%   D) 25%

38.

A

39. In cents, the attainable sums are 1, 2, 5, 6, 7, 10, 11, 12, 15, 16, 17, ..., 75, 76, 77. The only *unattainable* sums are those requiring 3 or 4 pennies; there are 30 *unattainable* sums less than 77.

   A) 8   B) 12   C) 47   D) 77

39.

C

40. The cars approach each other at $40 + 50 = 90$ km/h. The cars will meet in $450 \div 90 = 5$ hours.

   A) 11.25 hours   B) 10 hours   C) 9 hours   D) 5 hours

40.

D

The end of the contest ☞ **8**

Solutions

1980-81 Annual 8th Grade Contest

Tuesday, February 11, 1981

8

Contest Information

- **Solutions** Turn the page for detailed contest solutions (written in the question boxes) and letter answers (written in the *Answers* column to the right of each question).

- **Scores** Please remember that *this is a contest, not a test*—and there is no "passing" or "failing" score. Few students score as high as 30 points (75% correct). Students with half that, 15 points, *should be commended!*

- **Answers & Rating Scale** Turn to page 90 for the letter answers to each question and the rating scale for this contest.

1. Use the units' digit of each number: $8 \times 2 = 16$, so C is correct,

   A) 2   B) 4   C) 6   D) 8

   1. C

2. $4\frac{4}{5} = 4 + \frac{4}{5} = \frac{20}{5} + \frac{4}{5} = \frac{24}{5} = \frac{48}{5}$.

   A) $\frac{48}{10}$ B) $\frac{24}{10}$ C) $\frac{21}{5}$ D) 4.4

   2. A

3. $0.77 - 0.7 = 0.77 - 0.70 = 0.07$.

   A) 7.0   B) 0.7   C) 0.07   D) 0.007

   3. C

4. $6^2 = 36$, and $7^2 = 49$, and $(6.5)^2 = 42.25$, so $\sqrt{44} \approx 7$.

   A) 8   B) 7   C) 6   D) 5

   4. B

5. $\frac{1}{6} + \frac{1}{4} + \frac{1}{6} + \frac{1}{4} + \frac{1}{6} = (3 \times \frac{1}{6}) + (2 \times \frac{1}{4}) = \frac{3}{6} + \frac{2}{4} = \frac{1}{2} + \frac{1}{2} = 1$.

   A) $\frac{5}{26}$ B) $\frac{5}{24}$ C) $\frac{1}{2}$ D) 1

   5. D

6. 60 meters of fencing are needed to fence in a square lot. Each side is $60 \div 4 = 15$ m. The area of the lot is $15^2 = 225$ m^2.

   A) 3600 m^2 B) 900 m^2 C) 225 m^2 D) 15 m^2

   6. C

7. $(0.3)^2 = 0.3 \times 0.3 = 0.09$, so choice C is correct.

   A) 0.9   B) 0.6   C) 0.09   D) 0.06

   7. C

8. At 4:00 P.M., the hour hand is $4/12 = 1/3$ of the way around. Since $1/3$ of $360° = 120°$, choice B is correct.

   A) 110°   B) 120°   C) 135°   D) 150°

   8. B

9. $-2 - (-4) = -2 + 4 = 4 - 2 = 2$.

   A) 2   B) -2 C) 6   D) -6

   9. A

10. $(4 \times 5 \times 6) \times (\frac{1}{4} \times \frac{1}{5} \times \frac{1}{6}) = (4 \times \frac{1}{4}) \times (5 \times \frac{1}{5}) \times (6 \times \frac{1}{6}) = 1 \times 1 \times 1 = 1$.

    A) 0   B) 1   C) 3   D) 120

    10. B

11. $43.416 \div 0.06 = 4341.6 \div 6 = 723.6$.

    A) 7236.0   B) 723.6   C) 72.36   D) 7.236

    11. B

12. The ratio of girls to boys at a school dance was 3 to 2. If there were 30 boys at the dance, then there were $3/2 \times 30 = 45$ girls.

    A) 12   B) 18   C) 20   D) 45

    12. D

13. The numbers in the sequence are $1^2, 2^2, 3^2, 4^2, 5^2, 6^2, 7^2, 8^2, \ldots$

    A) 62   B) 63   C) 64   D) 66

    13. C

14. Since 9876 is even and divisible by 3, 2, 3, & 6 are all factors.

    A) 2   B) 3   C) 6   D) 7

    14. D

15. $0.125 \times 80 = 1/8 \times 80 = 10$, so choice D is correct.

    A) 0.1   B) 6.4   C) 8   D) 10

    15. D

Go on to the next page ⟱ **8**

	Answers
16. $\frac{1\frac{1}{2}}{15} = \frac{1.5}{15} = \frac{15}{150} = \frac{1}{10}$, so the missing number is 1. A) ½ B) 1 C) 1½ D) 2¼	16. B
17. $16 = 2 \times 8$ and $24 = 3 \times 8$; so the least common multiple is 6×8. A) 4 B) 8 C) 48 D) 384	17. C
18. The smallest primes are 2 and 3; their sum is 5, which is > 3. A) a multiple of 4 B) even C) more than 3 D) odd	18. C
19. $3/5 = 0.60$ & $2/3 = 0.666 \ldots$, so choice C is largest. A) $\frac{3}{5}$ B) $\frac{2}{3}$ C) 0.67 D) 0.669	19. C
20. A car left from Uphere at 9:00 A.M. and arrived at Downthere, 340 km away, at 1:15 P.M. the same day. The trip took 4¼ hr. The average speed of the car is $340 \div 4\frac{1}{4} = 340 \div 4.25$. A) $\frac{340}{7.75}$ B) $\frac{340}{255}$ C) $\frac{340}{415}$ D) $\frac{340}{4.25}$	20. D
21. The ratio of the diameters is 1:4. If the original diameters were 2 and 8, the radii would be 1 and 4; ratio is *still* 1:4. A) 1:2 B) 1:4 C) 1:8 D) 1:16	21. B
22. 25% of 50% of $100 = \frac{1}{4} \times \frac{1}{2} \times 100 = \frac{1}{4} \times 50 = 12\frac{1}{2}$. A) 12½ B) 25 C) 50 D) 75	22. A
23. Concentric circles have same center. Distance between them is the difference between their *radii*. Distance $= 4 - 3 = 1$. A) 0 B) 1 C) 2 D) 14	23. B
24. $3^3 \times 4^3 = (3 \times 4)^3 = 12^3$. A) 12^3 B) 12^6 C) 12^9 D) 5^3	24. A
25. An equilateral triangle and a regular hexagon share a common side. The perimeter of the triangle is 20 cm , so its side is 20/3. The perimeter of the hexagon is $6 \times 20/3 = 2 \times 20 = 40$ cm. A) 20 cm B) 40 cm C) 60 cm D) 120 cm	25. B
26. Since $\frac{2}{3} \times \frac{3}{2} = 1$ and $\frac{2}{3} \blacksquare \frac{3}{2} = 1$, $\blacksquare$ must really represent $\times$. A) $\times$ B) $\div$ C) $+$ D) $-$	26. A
27. If a equals its own reciprocal, $a = 1$ or -1; so $a^2 = 1$. A) -1 B) 4 C) 0 D) 1	27. D
28. On a certain test, six students scored 75, seven scored 80, eight scored 85, and nine scored 90. The overall average is $(6 \times 75 + 7 \times 80 + 8 \times 85 + 9 \times 90) \div (6 + 7 + 8 + 9) = 2500 \div 30 = 83\frac{1}{3}$. A) 80 B) 82½ C) 83⅓ D) 84	28. C

Go on to the next page ⫸ **8**

75

29. $\sqrt{\frac{1}{4}} + \sqrt{\frac{9}{4}} = \frac{1}{2} + \frac{3}{2} = \frac{4}{2} = 2 = \sqrt{4}$. A) $\sqrt{2}$ B) $\sqrt{\frac{5}{2}}$ C) $\sqrt{4}$ D) $\sqrt{\frac{9}{16}}$	29. C
30. Since 2^{99} and $(-2)^{99}$ are opposites, their sum is $0 = 0^{99}$. A) 0^{99} B) 2^{99} C) 2^{198} D) 4^{99}	30. A
31. $\angle P$ and $\angle Q$ are supplementary. Since $180° \div 5 = 36°$, $m\angle Q = 36°$ and $m\angle P = 144°$. A) $110°$ B) $116°$ C) $125°$ D) $144°$	31. D
32. $\frac{1}{2} + \frac{1}{3} = \frac{5}{6}$. The reciprocal of $\frac{5}{6}$ is $\frac{6}{5} = 6 \div 5 = 1.2$. A) 5 B) 2.5 C) 1.2 D) 0.866	32. C
33. The area of a right triangle is $\frac{1}{2} \times$ product of legs. Area's 30 cm^2, so product of legs is 60. Length of other leg is $60 \div 5 = 12$ cm. A) 6 cm B) 12 cm C) 18 cm D) 24 cm	33. B
34. $2 \times 4 \times 6 \times 8 = 2 \times 1 \times 2 \times 2 \times 2 \times 3 \times 2 \times 4 = 2^4 \times 1 \times 2 \times 3 \times 4$, so n is 16. A) 2 B) 4 C) 8 D) 16	34. D
35. A 1 ft $\times$ 3 inch $\times$ 4 inch rectangular block of ice melts at an average rate of 1 cubic inch per hour. Its volume is $12 \times 3 \times 4 = 144$ cubic inches and it is totally melted in 144 hours. A) 8 hrs. B) 12 hrs. C) 144 hrs. D) 152 hrs.	35. C
36. 4 hours $= 60 \times 60 \times 4 = 14400$ sec; $8/14400 = 1/1800 = (1/18)\%$. A) 2% B) $\frac{1}{2}\%$ C) $\frac{1}{9}\%$ D) $\frac{1}{18}\%$	36. D
37. Since $4 \times 15000 = 60000$ & $60000 \div 10000 = 6$, we need *at least* 6 tires. At 5000, rotate 2 tires with spares. After another 5000 miles, 2 tires have gone 10000 miles and are worn out. Replace them with the tires that have already gone 5000 miles. A) 1 B) 2 C) 4 D) 6	37. B
38. Every fourth term $(4 \times 12, 8 \times 12, 12 \times 12,$ & $16 \times 12)$ is a multiple of 16 since both factors in each product are multiples of 4. A) 1 B) 2 C) 4 D) 8	38. C
39. $1 + 2 + 3 + \ldots + 99 + 100 = 5050$; $(1 + 3 + 5 + \ldots + 197 + 199) = 2 \times$ $(1 + 2 + 3 + \ldots + 99 + 100) - (1 + 1 + 1 + \ldots + 1 + 1) = 10100 - 100$. A) 10000 B) 10050 C) 10100 D) 10150	39. A
40. d dimes $= 2d$ nickels, so d dimes $+ n$ nickels $= (2d + n)$ nickels. A) $(2d + n)$ nickels B) $(d + 2n)$ nickels C) $(10d + n)$ pennies D) $(d + 5n)$ pennies	40. A

The end of the contest ✍ **8**

Solutions

1981-82 Annual 8th Grade Contest

Tuesday, February 9, 1982

8

Contest Information

- **Solutions** Turn the page for detailed contest solutions (written in the question boxes) and letter answers (written in the *Answers* column to the right of each question).

- **Scores** Please remember that *this is a contest, not a test*—and there is no "passing" or "failing" score. Few students score as high as 30 points (75% correct). Students with half that, 15 points, *should be commended!*

- **Answers & Rating Scale** Turn to page 91 for the letter answers to each question and the rating scale for this contest.

1. $111 \times 999 = 111 \times (1000 - 1) = 111\,000 - 111 = 110\,889.$ A) $99\,999$ B) $109\,889$ C) $109\,989$ D) $110\,889$	1. D
2. The smallest sum is $100\,000 + 100\,000 = 200\,000$ and the largest sum is $999\,999 + 999\,999 = 1\,999\,999$; so choice B is correct. A) 5 digits B) 7 digits C) 8 digits D) 12 digits	2. B
3. $8.8 - 0.88 = 8.80 - 0.88 = 7.92.$ A) 0 B) 7.92 C) 8 D) 8.02	3. B
4. 5% of $\$25 = 0.05 \times \$25 = \$1.25.$ A) \$5 B) \$2.50 C) \$1.25 D) 50¢	4. C
5. $\frac{3}{4} = 3 \div 4 = 0.75$, so choice C is correct. A) 0.3 B) 0.6 C) 0.75 D) 0.8	5. C
6. The measure of one base angle in an isosceles triangle is $20°$. The measure of the largest angle is $180° - (2 \times 20°) = 140°$. A) $20°$ B) $90°$ C) $140°$ D) $160°$	6. C
7. $49 \div 0.7 = 490 \div 7 = 70$, so choice C is correct. A) 7 B) 10 C) 70 D) 140	7. C
8. $[(-1) + 2] + [(-3) + 4] + [(-5) + 6] + [(-7) + 8] + [(-9) + 10] = 5.$ A) -3 B) 0 C) 4 D) 5	8. D
9. The thousandths' digit of 0.03456 is 4, so round down to 0.03. A) 0.03 B) 0.04 C) 0.034 D) 0.035	9. A
10. 3600 seconds $= (3600 \div 60)$ minutes $= 60$ minutes $= 1$ hour. 1 hour from 9 A.M. is 10 A.M. A) 10 A.M. B) 11 A.M. C) 1 P.M. D) 2 P.M.	10. A
11. $(87 \times 96) - (85 \times 96) = (87 - 85) \times 96 = 2 \times 96 = 192.$ A) 2 B) 182 C) 192 D) 202	11. C
12. $4\frac{1}{6} \times 1\frac{4}{5} = \frac{25}{6} \times \frac{9}{5} = \frac{25 \times 9}{6 \times 5} = \frac{5 \times 3}{2 \times 1} = \frac{15}{2} = 7\frac{1}{2}.$ A) $4\frac{2}{15}$ B) $5\frac{29}{30}$ C) $7\frac{1}{6}$ D) $7\frac{1}{2}$	12. D
13. $2 + 2 \times 2 - 2 = 2 + (2 \times 2) - 2 = 2 + 4 - 2 = 4.$ A) 0 B) 2 C) 4 D) 6	13. C
14. Since 2 pounds $= 32$ ounces and the pizza is cut into 8 congruent pieces, the weight of three slices is $(32 \div 8) \times 3 = 12$ ounces. A) 3 ounces B) 6 ounces C) 8 ounces D) 12 ounces	14. D
15. $87\frac{1}{2}\% = 87.5\% = 0.875 = \frac{875}{1000} = \frac{175}{200} = \frac{7}{8}.$ A) $\frac{1}{6}$ B) $\frac{7}{8}$ C) $\frac{2}{3}$ D) $\frac{5}{9}$	15. B

Go on to the next page ⫸ **8**

		Answers
16.	$\dfrac{20 \times 30 \times 40 \times 50}{2 \times 3 \times 4 \times 5} = \dfrac{20}{2} \times \dfrac{30}{3} \times \dfrac{40}{4} \times \dfrac{50}{5} = 10 \times 10 \times 10 \times 10 = 10\,000.$ A) 10 B) 40 C) 1 000 D) 10 000	16. D
17.	$\dfrac{1}{3} - \dfrac{1}{2} = \dfrac{2}{6} - \dfrac{3}{6} = \dfrac{2-3}{6} = -\dfrac{1}{6}.$ A) $-\dfrac{1}{6}$ B) $\dfrac{1}{6}$ C) $-\dfrac{5}{6}$ D) $\dfrac{5}{6}$	17. A
18.	Perimeter is 2, so each side is $2 \div 4 = \frac{1}{2}$ and area is $(\frac{1}{2})^2 = \frac{1}{4}$. A) $\frac{1}{4}$ B) $\frac{1}{2}$ C) 1 D) $\sqrt{2}$	18. A
19.	Use units' digits: $3 \times 6 \times 9 = 162$, so units' digit is 2. A) 44 253 429 B) 44 253 431 C) 44 253 432 D) 44 253 433	19. C
20.	Since 5 cm represents 40 meters, 1 cm represents $40 \div 5 =$ 8 meters and $6\frac{3}{4}$ cm represents $6\frac{3}{4} \times 8 = 54$ meters. A) 51 meters B) 54 meters C) 57 meters D) 60 meters	20. B
21.	$5^6 \times 2^6 = (5 \times 2)^6 = 10^6 = 1\,000\,000.$ A) 1 000 000 B) 10^{12} C) 7^6 D) 10 000 000	21. A
22.	If $p - 2$, p, and $p + 2$ are all primes, the *only* possible value of p is 5 since $5 - 2$, 5, and $5 + 2$ are all primes. A) 3 B) 5 C) 59 D) 89	22. B
23.	$\dfrac{1 - 0.50}{1 - 0.25} = \dfrac{0.50}{0.75} = \dfrac{50}{75} = \dfrac{2}{3}.$ A) $\frac{1}{8}$ B) $\frac{3}{8}$ C) $\frac{2}{3}$ D) 2	23. C
24.	The measures of a radius of a circle and a side of a square are equal. If each measure is 1, the area of the circle is π and the area of the square is 1. The ratio of the areas is $\pi{:}1$. A) 1:1 B) $2\pi{:}1$ C) $\pi{:}1$ D) $1{:}\pi$	24. C
25.	$\sqrt{3^2 + 4^2 + 12^2} = \sqrt{9 + 16 + 144} = \sqrt{169} = 13.$ A) 13 B) 19 C) 84 D) 169	25. A
26.	1% of 1% $= 1/100 \times 1/100 = 1/10\,000$, so number is 10 000. A) 100 B) 1 000 C) 10 000 D) 100 000	26. C
27.	The measure of the smallest angle can *never* be $> 60°$. A) $\frac{1}{2}°$ B) $10°$ C) $45°$ D) $61°$	27. D
28.	Sum of the measures of *all* the angles is $(6-2) \times 180°$; each is $120°$. A) $60°$ B) $120°$ C) $90°$ D) $30°$	28. B
29.	Sue's present age + 30 years $= 1\frac{1}{2}$ times her present age, so $\frac{1}{2}$ her present age is 30 and Sue is now $2 \times 30 = 60$ years old. A) 15 B) 20 C) 45 D) 60	29. D
30.	The cost of a tire and a jack is $110. If the tire cost $100 more than the jack, the jack cost $5 and the tire cost $105. A) $5 B) $10 C) $100 D) $105	30. A

Go on to the next page ⫸ **8**

31.	There are two numbers whose sum is 30 and whose product is 221. The numbers are 13 and 17; they differ by 4. A) 4 B) 3 C) 2 D) 1	31. A
32.	$\dfrac{3^{200}}{3^{50}} = 3^{200-50} = 3^{150}$. A) 4 B) 150 C) 3^4 D) 3^{150}	32. D
33.	It's like changing each side from a 1×1 square to a 2×2. There's 4 times as much area to paint. Since 1 liter is required to paint the smaller block, 4 liters are required to paint the larger block. A) 2 B) 4 C) 6 D) 8	33. B
34.	The second hand goes once around the clock each *minute*, not each second. In 60 minutes, it goes $60 \times 10\pi = 600\pi$ cm. A) 600π cm B) 3600π cm C) 6000π cm D) 36000π cm	34. A
35.	One skip = 4 hops, and 1 jump = 2 skips = 8 hops. A hop, skip, and a jump = $1 + 4 + 8 = 13$ hops. A) 7 B) 8 C) 12 D) 13	35. D
36.	Since $3^2 = 2^3 + 1$, $a = 3$ and $b = 2$. The value of $(a + b)^2$ is $(3 + 2)^2 = 5^2 = 25$. A) 9 B) 25 C) 36 D) 49	36. B
37.	A dog weighs $\frac{4}{5}$ of its weight plus 40 pounds, so $\frac{1}{5}$ of its weight is 40 pound. Thus, the dog weighs $5 \times 40 = 200$ pounds. A) 48 pounds B) 72 pounds C) 160 pounds D) 200 pounds	37. D
38.	The diagram shows how to divide the garden. The inner square is 2 m $\times$ 2 m; each surrounding rectangle is 4 m $\times$ 6 m. A) 3 m $\times$ 3 m B) 8 m $\times$ 3 m C) 4 m $\times$ 6 m D) 2 m $\times$ 12 m	38. C
39.	The owl went up 18 units each day and down 13 units each night. By night 14, the owl's net movement was 70 units. On day 15, the owl climbed to 88 units; at night it fell back to 75. It got to 93 units on day 16, its *first* time at the top. A) day 16 B) day 17 C) day 18 D) day 19	39. A
40.	Since 20 miles takes 20 mins at 60 mph, and 30 mins at 40 mph, it took 50 mins to go 40 miles. Average rate = (total distance)÷ (total time), so average rate is 40 miles÷5/6 hrs = 48 mph. A) 50 B) 48 C) 47 D) 46	40. B

The end of the contest ✍ **8**

Answer Keys &
Difficulty Ratings

●●●●●●●●●●●●●●●●●

1977-78 through 1981-82

ANSWERS, 1977-78 7th Grade Contest

1. D	9. C	17. D	25. C	33. A
2. B	10. A	18. B	26. C	34. C
3. D	11. A	19. B	27. B	35. D
4. D	12. C	20. B	28. D	36. D
5. A	13. C	21. D	29. A	37. B
6. A	14. D	22. C	30. D	38. A
7. C	15. A	23. A	31. B	39. B
8. C	16. A	24. C	32. B	40. B

RATE YOURSELF!!!
for the 1977-78 7th GRADE CONTEST

Score	Rating
34-40	Another Einstein
31-33	Mathematical Wizard
28-30	School Champion
25-27	Grade Level Champion
22-24	Best In The Class
19-21	Excellent Student
16-18	Good Student
13-15	Average Student
0-12	Better Luck Next Time

ANSWERS, 1978-79 7th Grade Contest

1. D	9. C	17. D	25. D	33. D
2. C	10. C	18. B	26. C	34. A
3. A	11. A	19. B	27. A	35. C
4. B	12. D	20. C	28. D	36. D
5. B	13. D	21. A	29. B	37. B
6. A	14. B	22. C	30. D	38. A
7. B	15. D	23. C	31. C	39. A
8. A	16. C	24. C	32. B	40. C

RATE YOURSELF!!!
for the 1978-79 7th GRADE CONTEST

Score	Rating
36-40	Another Einstein
33-35	Mathematical Wizard
31-32	School Champion
28-30	Grade Level Champion
25-27	Best In The Class
22-24	Excellent Student
19-21	Good Student
16-18	Average Student
0-15	Better Luck Next Time

ANSWERS, 1979-80 7th Grade Contest

1. B	9. B	17. A	25. D	33. D
2. C	10. C	18. B	26. D	34. B
3. A	11. B	19. C	27. A	35. D
4. D	12. B	20. B	28. D	36. C
5. D	13. C	21. D	29. A	37. C
6. C	14. A	22. A	30. B	38. B
7. A	15. B	23. C	31. C	39. A
8. A	16. D	24. C	32. B	40. C

RATE YOURSELF!!!
for the 1979-80 7th GRADE CONTEST

Score	Rating
35-40	Another Einstein
32-34	Mathematical Wizard
29-31	School Champion
27-28	Grade Level Champion
24-26	Best In The Class
21-23	Excellent Student
18-20	Good Student
14-17	Average Student
0-13	Better Luck Next Time

ANSWERS, 1980-81 7th Grade Contest

1. D	9. B	17. A	25. A	33. D
2. A	10. D	18. B	26. D	34. D
3. B	11. B	19. B	27. D	35. B
4. C	12. A	20. B	28. C	36. C
5. D	13. D	21. A	29. A	37. D
6. C	14. A	22. C	30. B	38. A
7. B	15. C	23. D	31. B	39. B
8. C	16. C	24. C	32. B	40. A

RATE YOURSELF!!!
for the 1980-81 7th GRADE CONTEST

Score	Rating
36-40	Another Einstein
33-35	Mathematical Wizard
30-32	School Champion
26-29	Grade Level Champion
23-25	Best In The Class
20-22	Excellent Student
17-19	Good Student
15-16	Average Student
0-14	Better Luck Next Time

ANSWERS, 1981-82 7th Grade Contest

1. C	9. A	17. B	25. A	33. C
2. B	10. B	18. D	26. D	34. D
3. B	11. D	19. A	27. B	35. D
4. D	12. C	20. D	28. A	36. D
5. C	13. B	21. D	29. D	37. B
6. C	14. C	22. D	30. C	38. C
7. B	15. C	23. B	31. A	39. D
8. B	16. A	24. A	32. C	40. A

RATE YOURSELF!!!
for the 1981-82 7th GRADE CONTEST

Score	Rating
38-40	Another Einstein
35-37	Mathematical Wizard
32-34	School Champion
29-31	Grade Level Champion
25-28	Best In The Class
22-24	Excellent Student
20-21	Good Student
17-19	Average Student
0-16	Better Luck Next Time

ANSWERS, 1977-78 8th Grade Contest

1. C	9. B	17. A	25. D	33. A
2. D	10. A	18. B	26. C	34. A
3. D	11. A	19. B	27. B	35. D
4. A	12. C	20. B	28. D	36. A
5. C	13. B	21. D	29. A	37. B
6. A	14. D	22. C	30. D	38. B
7. C	15. D	23. A	31. B	39. B
8. C	16. A	24. D	32. B	40. C

RATE YOURSELF!!!
for the 1977-78 8th GRADE CONTEST

Score	Rating
35-40	Another Einstein
32-34	Mathematical Wizard
29-31	School Champion
26-28	Grade Level Champion
24-25	Best In The Class
21-23	Excellent Student
18-20	Good Student
14-17	Average Student
0-13	Better Luck Next Time

ANSWERS, 1978-79 8th Grade Contest

1. B	9. B	17. B	25. D	33. C
2. B	10. D	18. C	26. D	34. B
3. A	11. C	19. C	27. C	35. A
4. A	12. A	20. A	28. D	36. B
5. C	13. A	21. C	29. A	37. A
6. A	14. C	22. A	30. B	38. A
7. A	15. D	23. B	31. B	39. C
8. D	16. D	24. D	32. A	40. A

RATE YOURSELF!!!
for the 1978-79 8th GRADE CONTEST

Score		Rating
37-40		Another Einstein
35-36		Mathematical Wizard
32-34		School Champion
29-31		Grade Level Champion
26-28		Best In The Class
22-25		Excellent Student
20-21		Good Student
16-19		Average Student
0-15		Better Luck Next Time

ANSWERS, 1979-80 8th Grade Contest

1. A	9. A	17. B	25. C	33. D
2. B	10. D	18. B	26. D	34. B
3. A	11. C	19. D	27. A	35. C
4. C	12. B	20. D	28. D	36. C
5. C	13. A	21. B	29. B	37. C
6. D	14. D	22. A	30. A	38. A
7. A	15. C	23. C	31. B	39. C
8. D	16. B	24. C	32. B	40. D

RATE YOURSELF!!!
for the 1979-80 8th GRADE CONTEST

Score		Rating
37-40		**Another Einstein**
34-36		**Mathematical Wizard**
31-33		**School Champion**
28-30		**Grade Level Champion**
26-27		**Best In The Class**
23-25		**Excellent Student**
20-22		**Good Student**
16-19		**Average Student**
0-15		**Better Luck Next Time**

ANSWERS, 1980-81 8th Grade Contest

1. C	9. A	17. C	25. B	33. B
2. A	10. B	18. C	26. A	34. D
3. C	11. B	19. C	27. D	35. C
4. B	12. D	20. D	28. C	36. D
5. D	13. C	21. B	29. C	37. B
6. C	14. D	22. A	30. A	38. C
7. C	15. D	23. B	31. D	39. A
8. B	16. B	24. A	32. C	40. A

RATE YOURSELF!!!
for the 1980-81 8th GRADE CONTEST

Score	Rating
38-40	Another Einstein
35-37	Mathematical Wizard
31-34	School Champion
28-30	Grade Level Champion
25-27	Best In The Class
23-24	Excellent Student
21-22	Good Student
17-20	Average Student
0-16	Better Luck Next Time

ANSWERS, 1981-82 8th Grade Contest

1. D	9. A	17. A	25. A	33. D
2. B	10. A	18. A	26. C	34. A
3. B	11. C	19. C	27. D	35. D
4. C	12. D	20. B	28. B	36. B
5. C	13. C	21. A	29. D	37. D
6. C	14. D	22. B	30. A	38. C
7. C	15. B	23. C	31. A	39. A
8. D	16. D	24. C	32. D	40. B

RATE YOURSELF!!!
for the 1981-82 8th GRADE CONTEST

Score	Rating
38-40	Another Einstein
35-37	Mathematical Wizard
32-34	School Champion
29-31	Grade Level Champion
27-28	Best In The Class
24-26	Excellent Student
21-23	Good Student
17-20	Average Student
0-16	Better Luck Next Time

Middle Grades Math
Electronic Workbook CD-ROM
More features than an after-school program, without the high cost
(Level 1 for Grades 5-8, for Windows 3.1 or later)

Middle Grades Math Workbook is an electronic tutor right at your side. All year long, get the help you need, just when you want it! Great for end-of-the-year review! *Middle Grades Math* workbook is an **electronic workbook, not a game**.

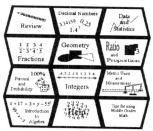

A User-Friendly Interface makes this powerful tool easy to use.

Built-in Help sections are linked to all problem sets. You can use *Help* to get definitions, sample problems, and solutions.

Answers, detailed solutions, or full explanations are given for all problems—but only after you first enter your answer.

Report Writer keeps track of which problems were answered incorrectly, what answer was given, the correct answer, and other statistics of student progress for each day's problems.

Minimum System Requirements: 386-based computer (486 or higher recommended); hard disk with minimum 10 MB free space; Windows 3.1 or 3.11, Windows 95, or Windows NT 3.51 or later; 8 MB memory for Windows 3.1 or 3.11, or Windows 95; 16 MB of memory for Windows NT 3.51; a CD-ROM drive; a VGA monitor displaying 256 colors under Windows.

CD-ROM $39.95 ($49.95 Canadian) + $5 S&H. Network Lic $5 each computer

Use the form below (or a copy) to order your CD-ROM

Your Name: _____

School Name (if applicable): _____

Address: _____

City: _____ State: _____ Zip: _____

Middle Grades Math CD-ROM (or Province)   (or Postal Code)
 # copies @ $39.95 (U.S.) ____ + $5 Shipping/Handling Fee Total $_____

☐ Check or Purchase Order Enclosed; *or*

☐ Visa/MasterCard # _____

☐ Exp. Date _____ Signature _____

Mail your order with payment to:
Math League Press
P.O. Box 720
Tenafly, NJ USA 07670-0720
Phone: (201) 568-6328 • Fax: (201) 816-0125

Math League Contest Books
4th Grade Through High School Levels

Written by Steven R. Conrad and Daniel Flegler, recipients of President Reagan's 1985 Presidential Awards for Excellence in Mathematics Teaching, each book provides schools and students with:

- Easy-to-use format designed for a 30-minute period
- Problems ranging from straightforward to challenging
- Contests from 4th grade through high school

1-10 copies of any one book: $12.95 each ($16.95 Canadian)
11 or more copies of any one book: $9.95 each ($12.95 Canadian)

Use the form below (or a copy) to order your books

Name: _____

Address: _____

City: _____ State: _____ Zip: _____
                         (or Province)   (or Postal Code)

Available Titles	# of Copies	Cost
Math Contests—Grades 4, 5, 6		
Volume 1: 1979-80 through 1985-86	_____	_____
Volume 2: 1986-87 through 1990-91	_____	_____
Volume 3: 1991-92 through 1995-96	_____	_____
Math Contests—Grades 7 & 8		
Volume 1: 1977-78 through 1981-82	_____	_____
Volume 2: 1982-83 through 1990-91	_____	_____
Math Contests—7, 8, & Algebra Course 1		
Volume 3: 1991-92 through 1995-96	_____	_____
Math Contests—High School		
Volume 1: 1977-78 through 1981-82	_____	_____
Volume 2: 1982-83 through 1990-91	_____	_____
Volume 3: 1991-92 through 1995-96	_____	_____
Shipping and Handling		$3.00

Please allow 4-6 weeks for delivery   Total: $_____

☐ Check or Purchase Order Enclosed; **or**

☐ Visa / MasterCard # _____

☐ Exp. Date_____ Signature _____

Mail your order with payment to:
Math League Press
P.O. Box 720
Tenafly, NJ USA 07670
Phone: (201) 568-6328 • Fax: (201) 816-0125